Dedicated to
W.R.P. Diana

Intentionally Left Bank... er, Blank

Special thanks to

Stefany Reich-Silber
Ian Foti-Landis
Andrew Foti-Landis
Chase Foti-Landis
Rita Foti
Marie Joiner
Janet Levenson
Bradley Hilton
Cathi Hackbarth
Carole Ono
Mia Villanueva
Melanie Okamoto
Elaine Eger
Scott Cockrell
Jack Coglizer
Jane Kaer
Emil Brown
Forrest Lewis

"Jesus wept."

John 11, Verse 35

CRUDE AND UNUSUAL PUNISHMENT

by

T. A. Landis

BLUE FLASH PRESS

Mars Venus Earth ~~Pluto~~

Crude and Unusual Punishment

By T. A. Landis

Published by Blue Flash Press

ISBN : 978-0-615-42671-6
First Edition

ACIDIC JEWS

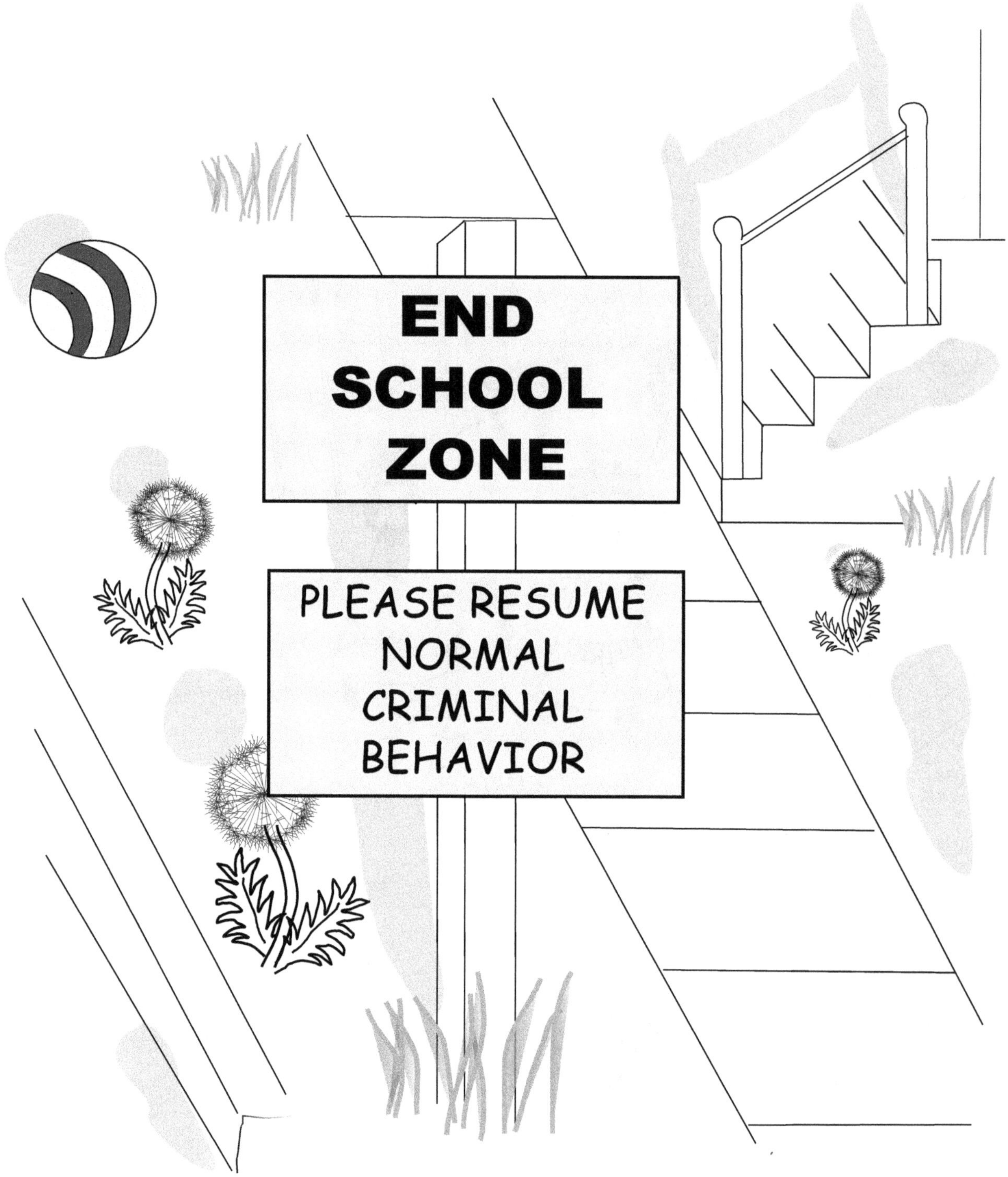
END
SCHOOL
ZONE
PLEASE RESUME
NORMAL
CRIMINAL
BEHAVIOR

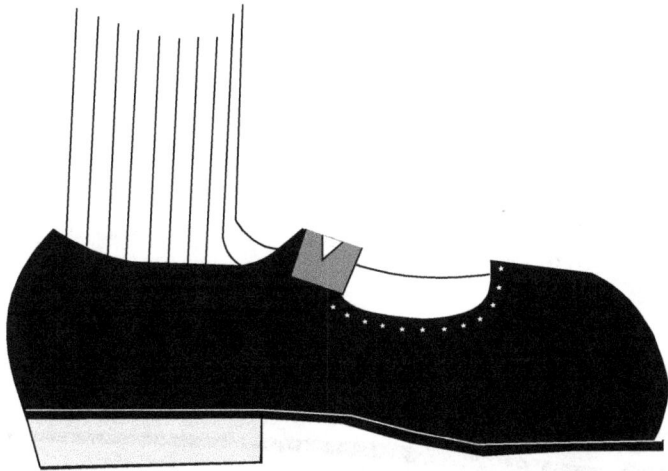

ATTACK OF THE 50 FOOT GIRL

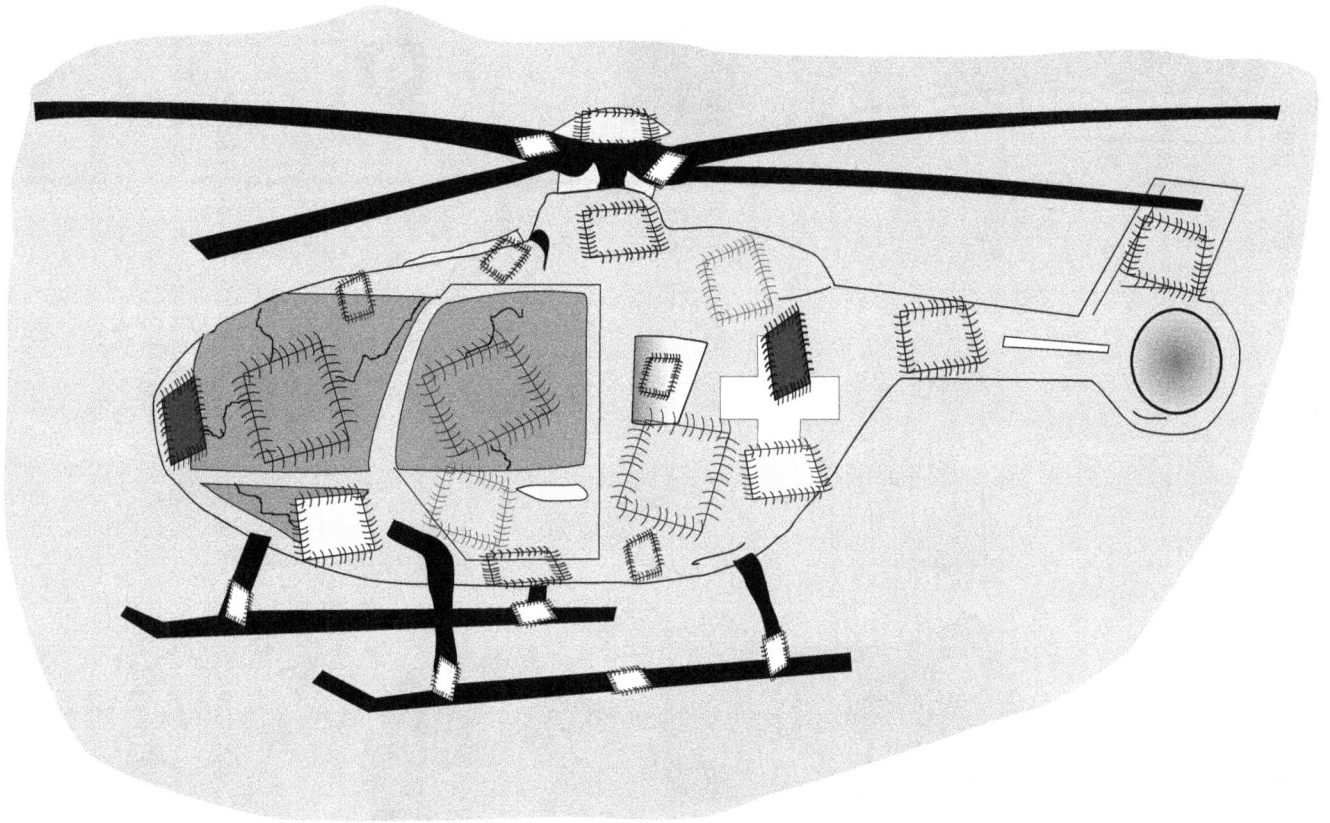

A PATCHY HELICOPTER

"The benefit of 1 pill of Resveratrol is equal to the benefits of drinking 1,000 bottles of red wine." Dr. Oz

THAT'SH NINE HUNDRED...
NINE HUNDERD...
NINE NINE NINE...
NINEY-SEVENNNNNNN...
NINETY...
NINEY NIGHTY...
NOONY...zzzzzzz

CARTOON BASICS #23:

HOW TO DRAW FAST

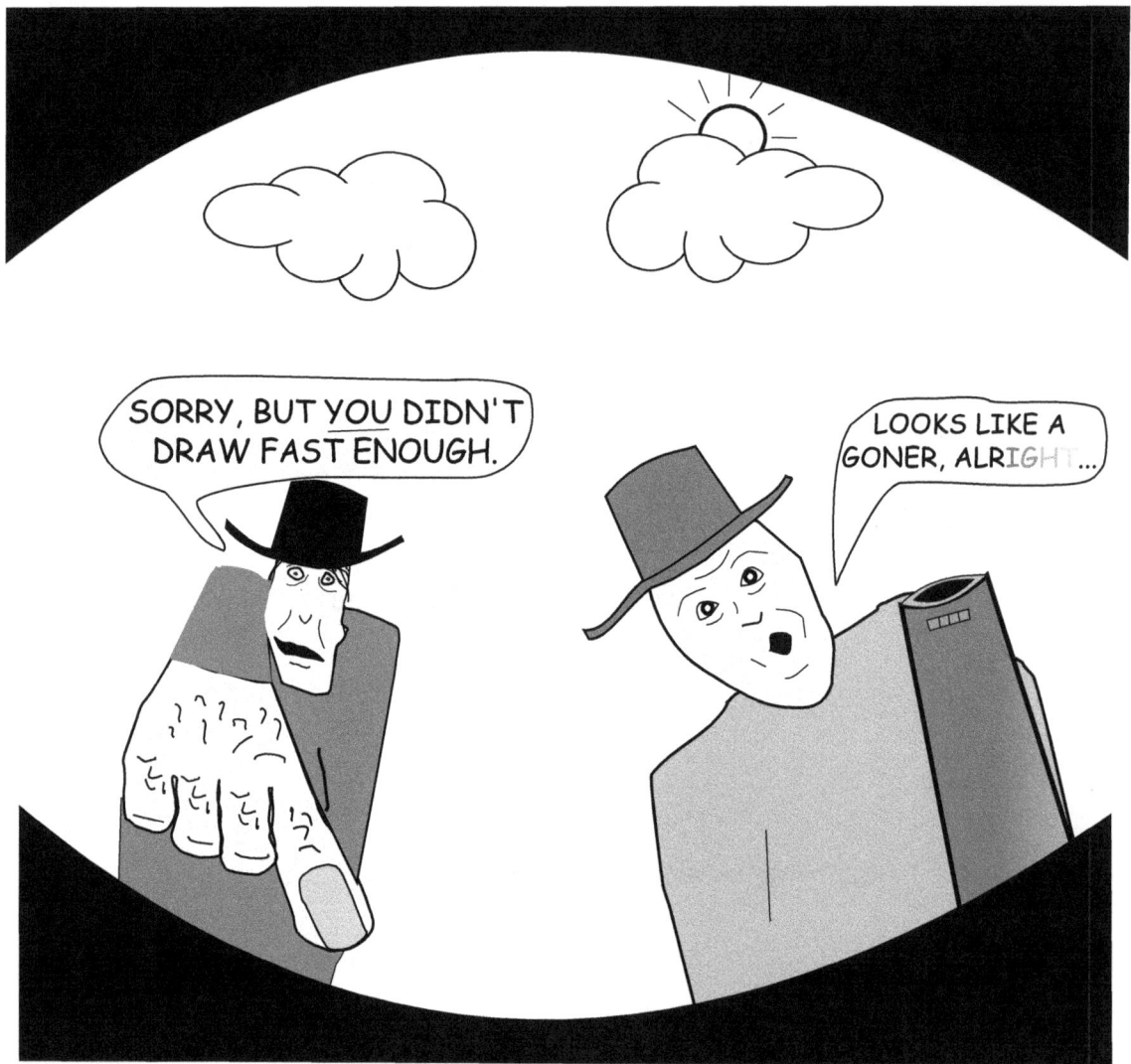

THOR HEYERDAHL'S GHOST, WISHING TO DUPLICATE HIS HISTORIC TRIP TO POLYNESIA, HAS HIS ZOMBIES MAKE HIS NEW VESSEL OUT OF ANTIQUES.

ANTIKI!

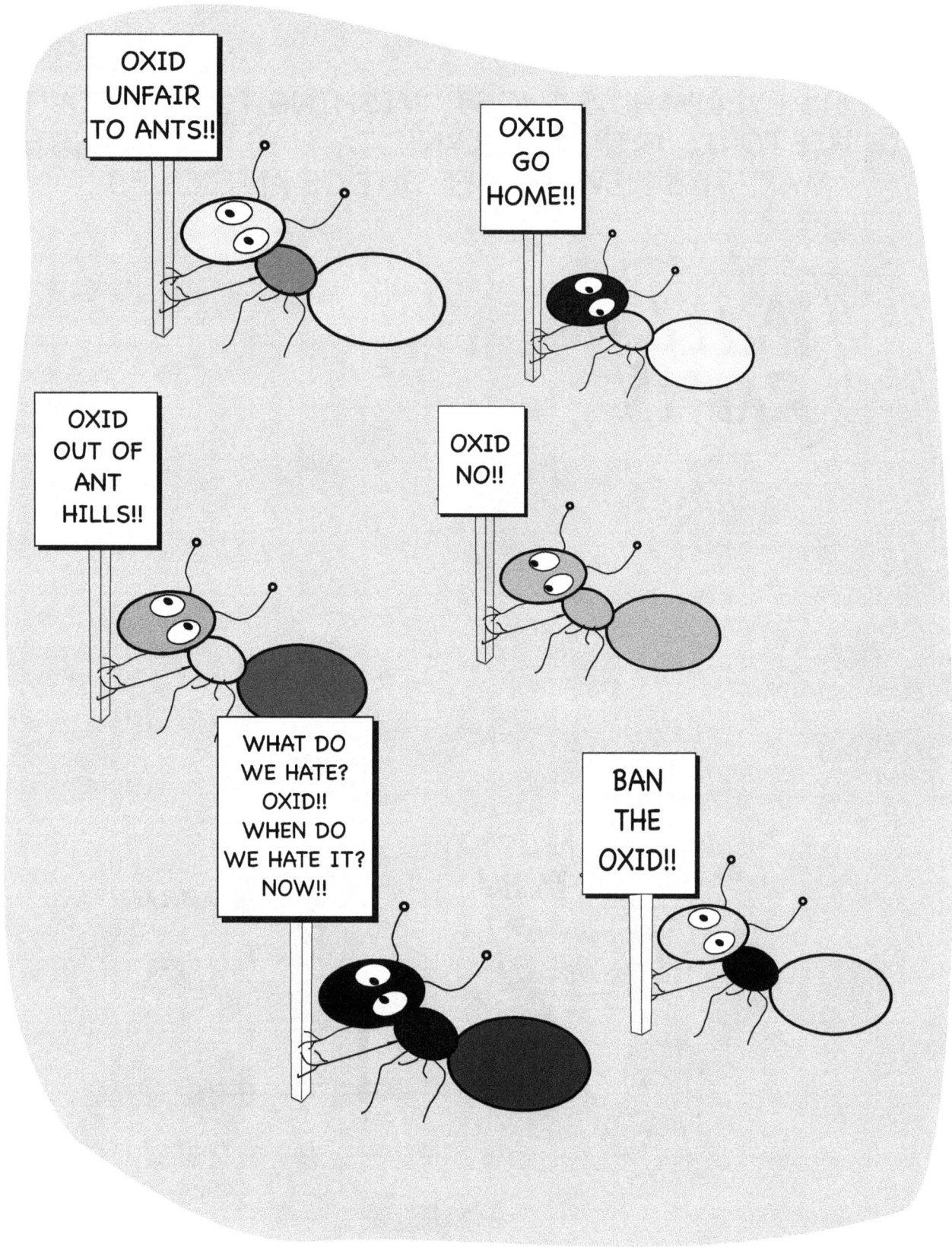

ANTIOXIDANTS

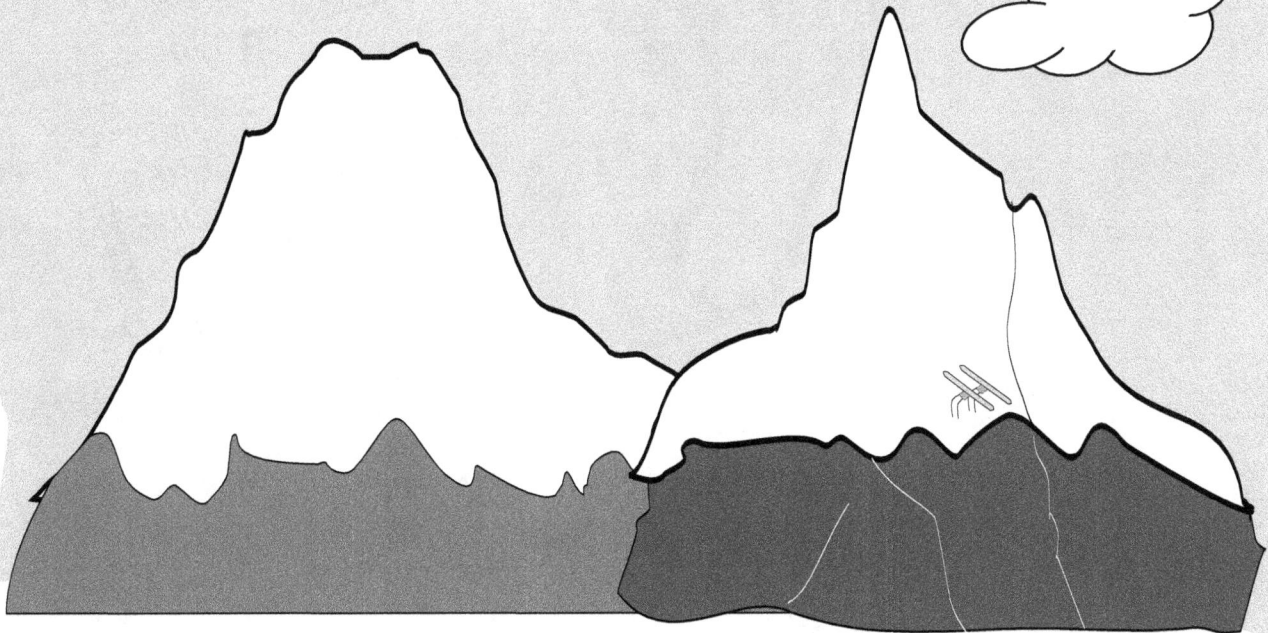

AFTER SOME HEATED DISCUSSION,
BOZO AND MOZART COME UP WITH
AN AGREEMENT THEY CAN BOTH LIVE WITH.

DRAWING A BLANK...

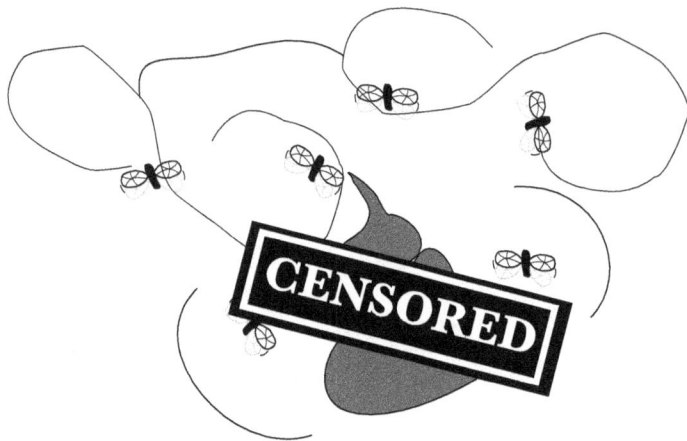

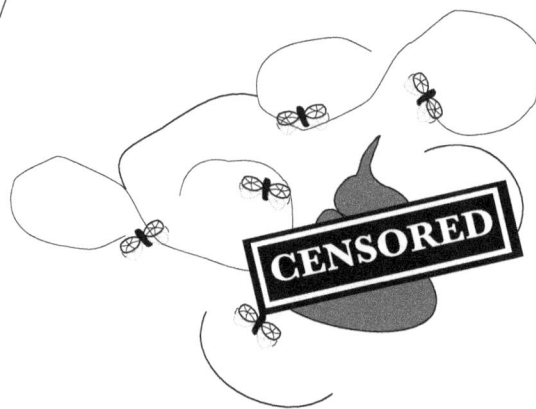

THE BUCCANEARS

"WELL MA, IT LOOKS LIKE
WE GOT US A BUMPER CROP!"

CARTOON BASICS #15:

HOW TO DRAW LIGHTNING

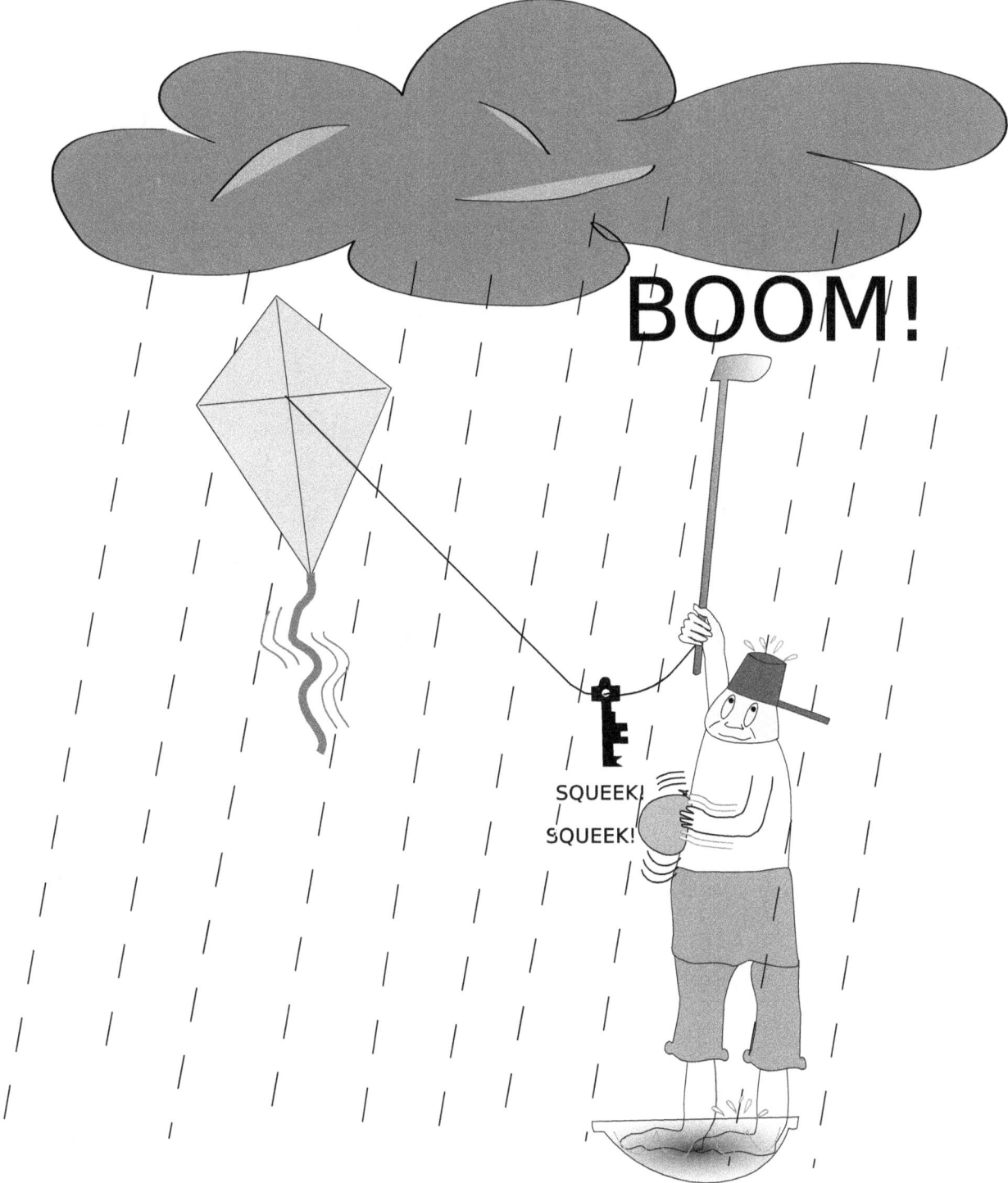

BOOM!

SQUEEK!

SQUEEK!

THE MATRIMONIAL GUIDE FOR CAVEMEN

DIVIDE AND CONK HER

UNCLEAR ON THE CONCEPT, "CHARIOT" TUBMAN
KEEPS LEAVING THE RUNAWAYS BEHIND

WAITING FOR YOUR JOB
INTERVIEW WITH THE CIRCUS

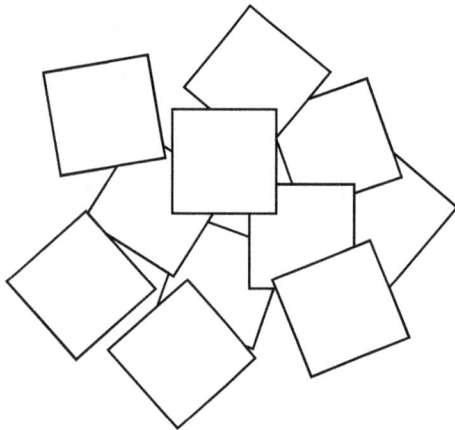

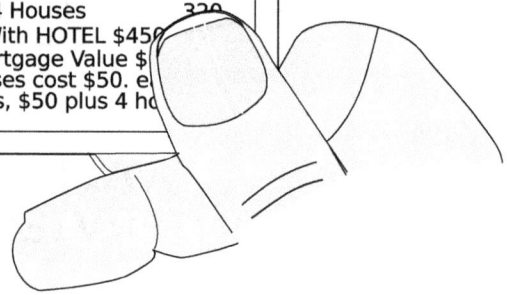

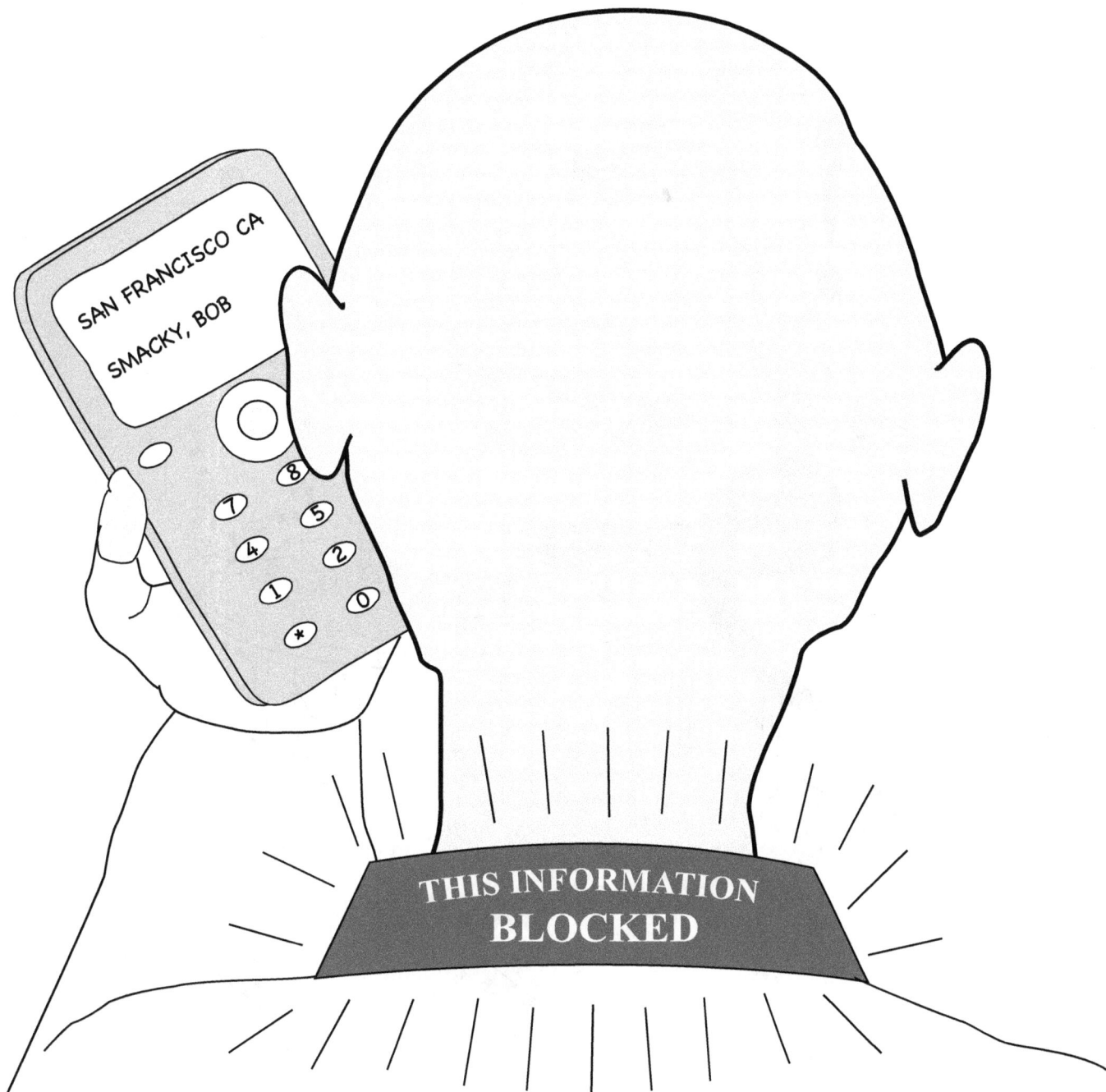

COLLAR ID

ACOMMADATING

COMPLIMENTARY TICKETS

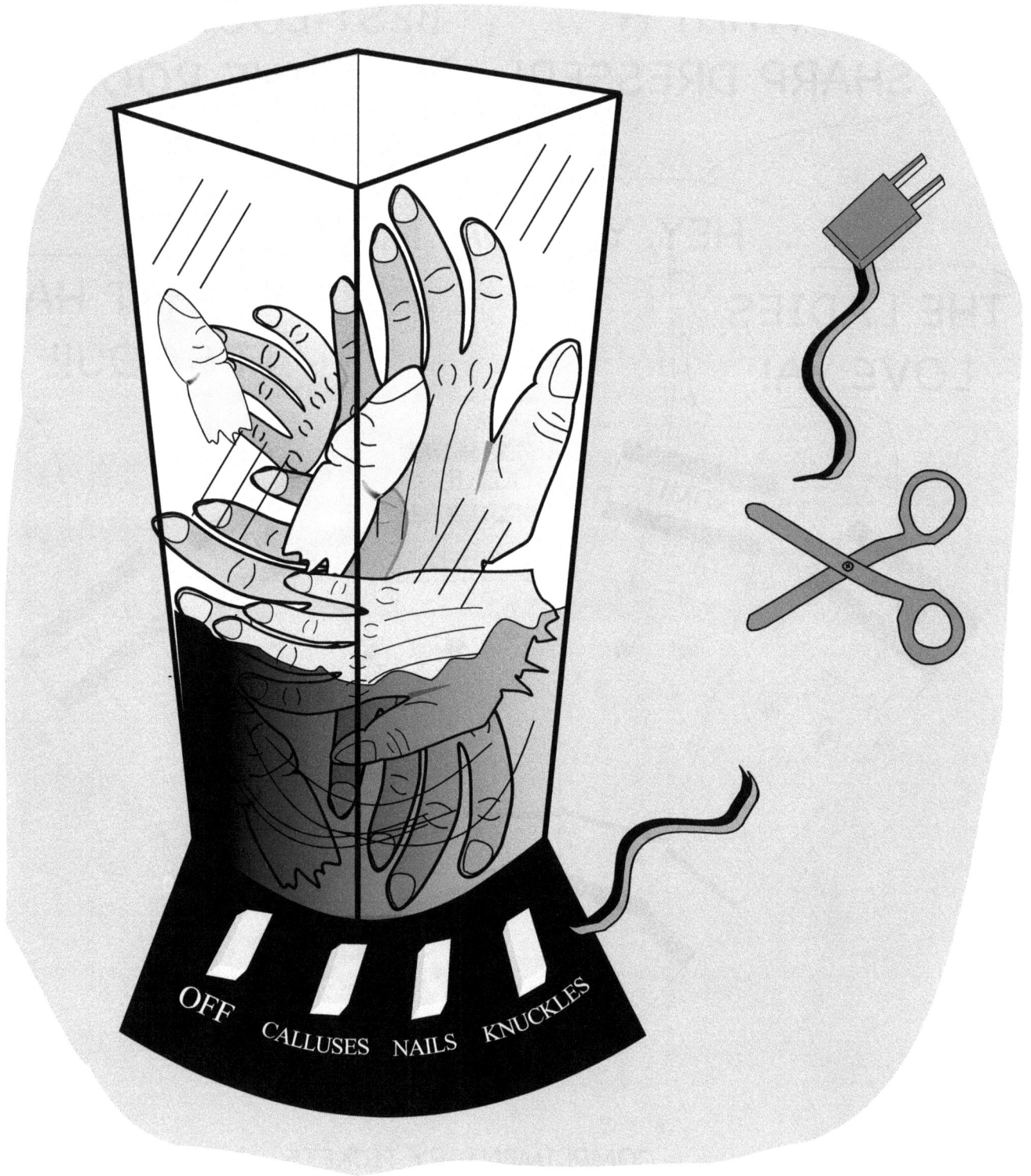

ARTIST'S CONCEPTION OF
THE CORDLESS HAND BLENDER

OFF   CALLUSES   NAILS   KNUCKLES

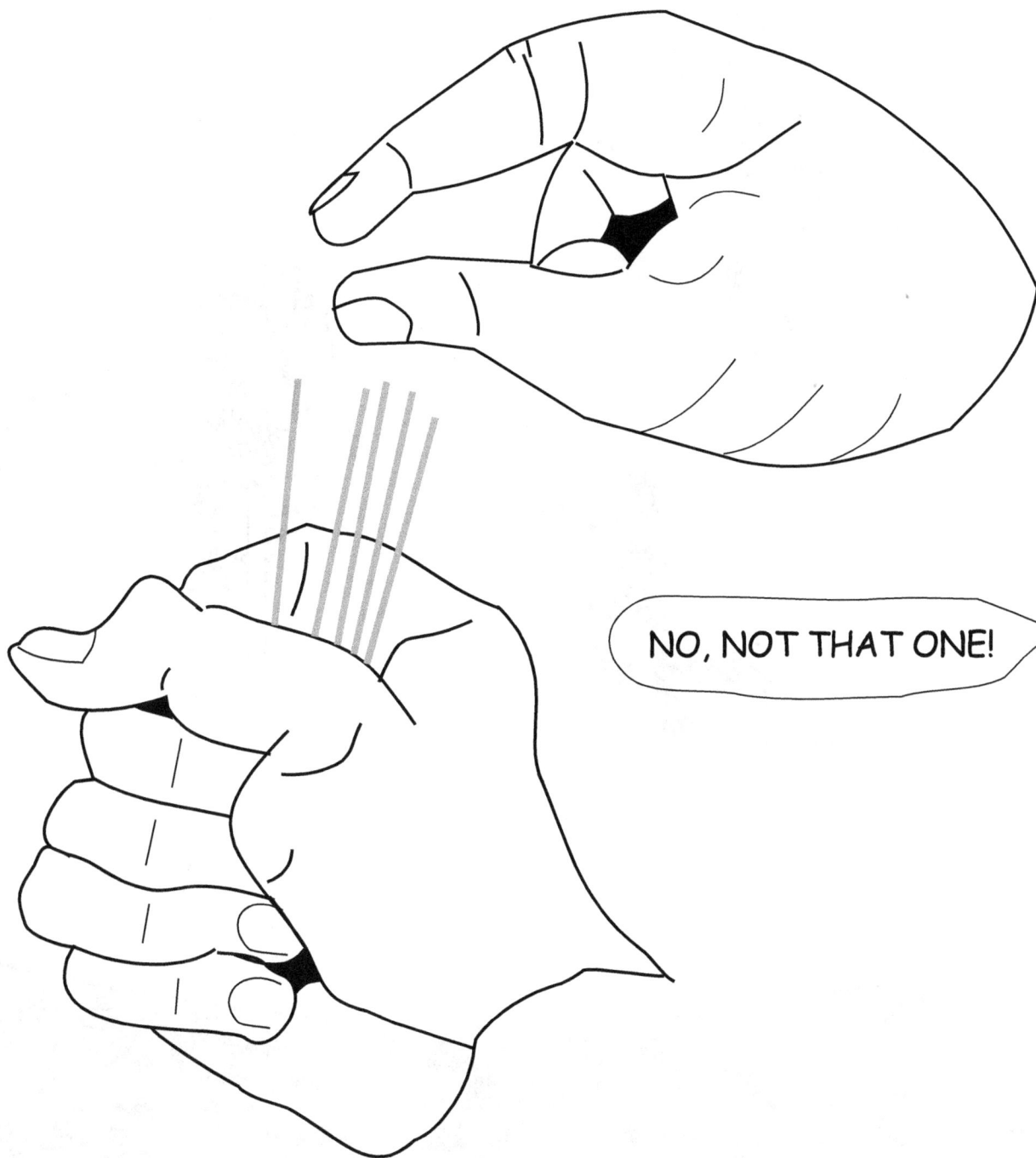

DANCING WITH THE STAIRS

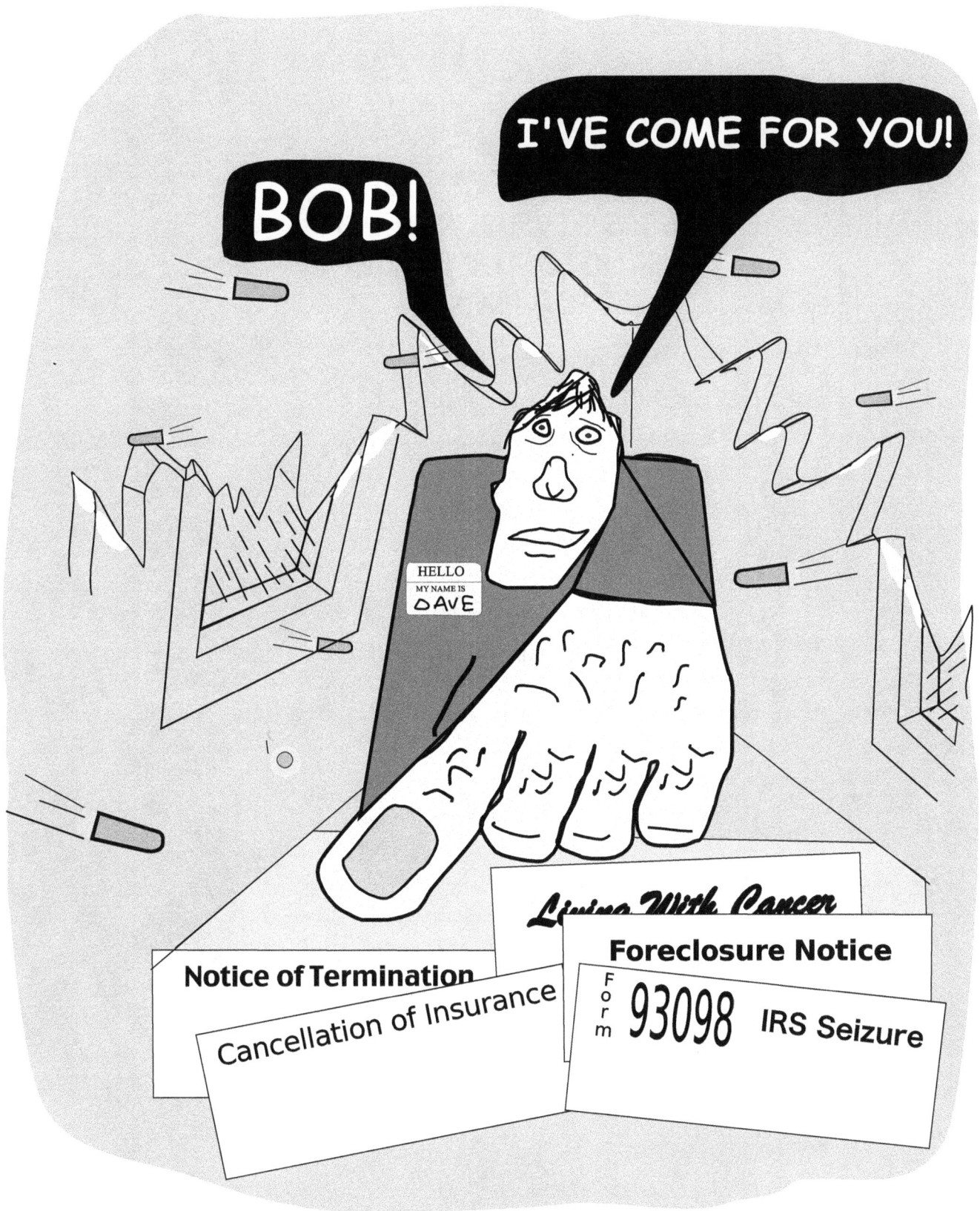

Bob was particularly disappointed by
the appearance of his Dave of Reckoning

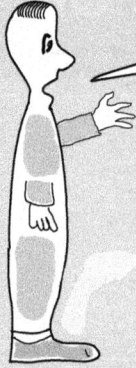

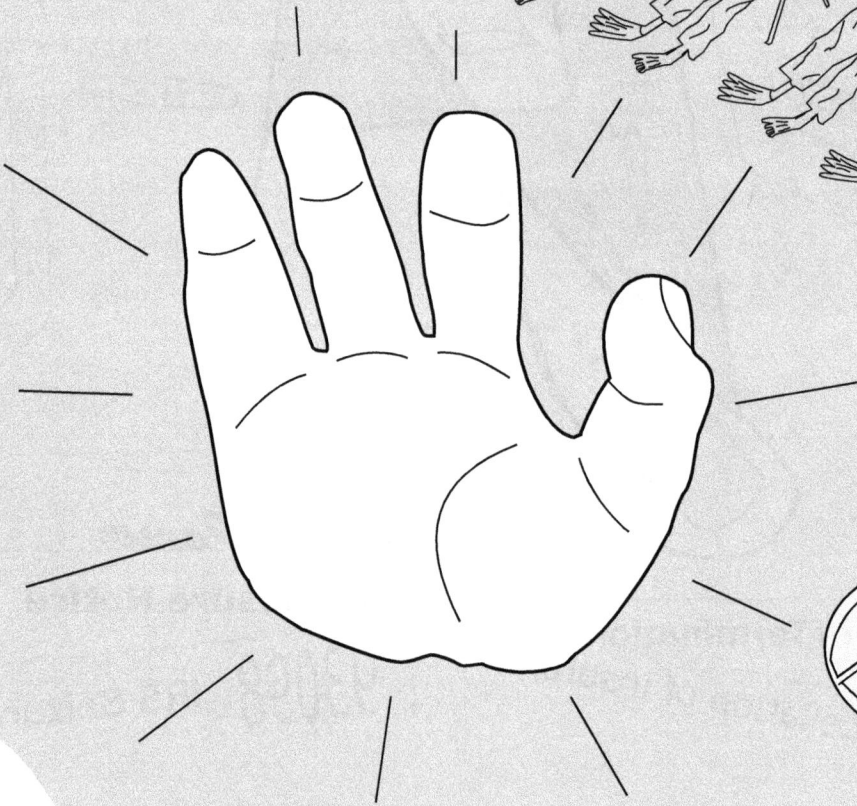

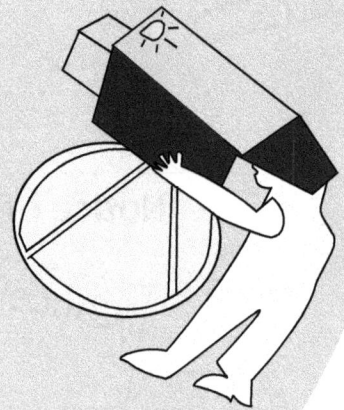

THUMP!

BAM!

CRACK!

SCRAAAAAATCH!

SLAM!

CRAAAAASH!

BOOM!

⸚\\\\\|////////
AAAAAHHHHHH!
///////|\\\\\⸚

DENTS FOG

DOGPHONES

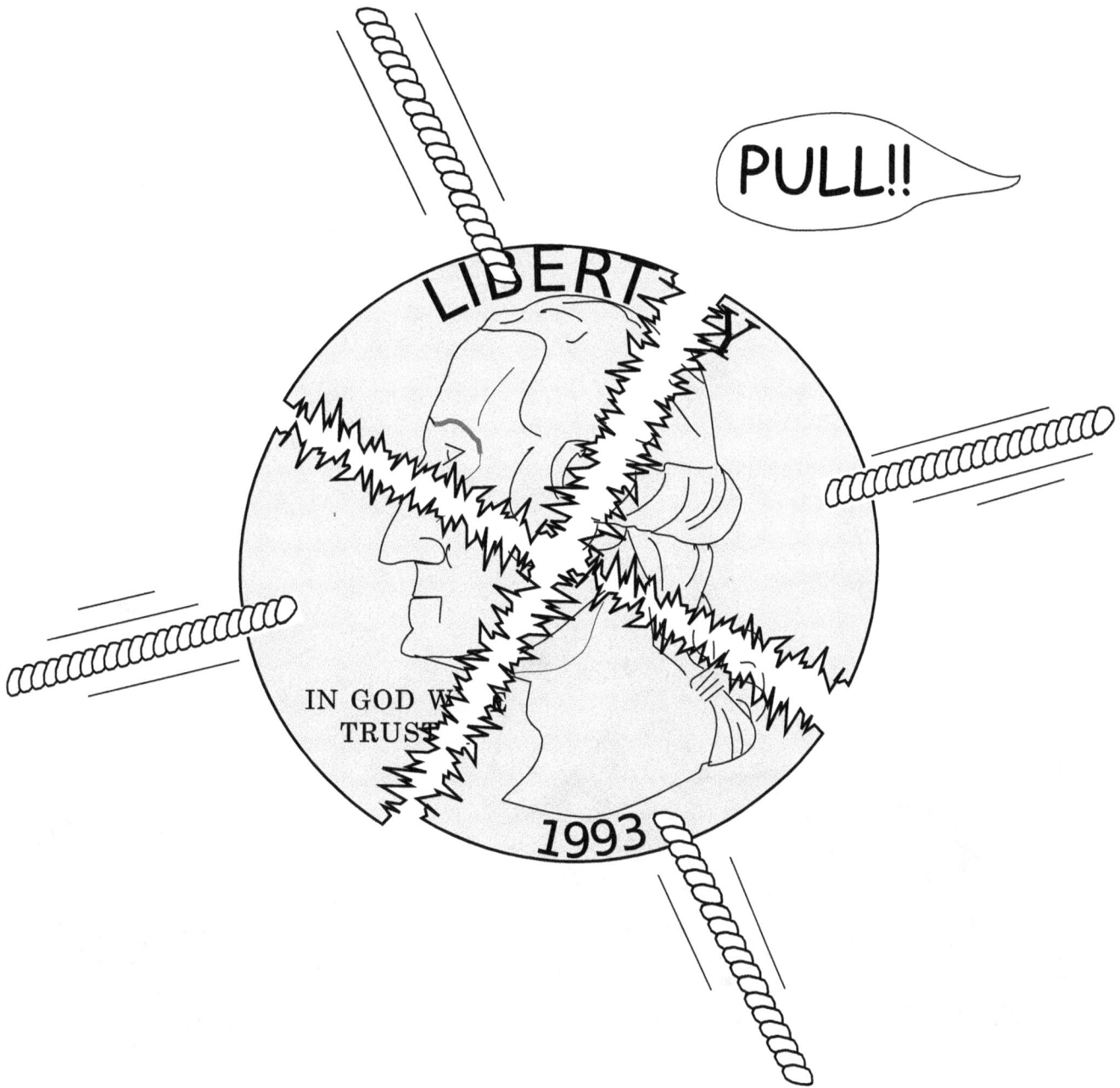

SITTIN' ON THE DUCK OF THE BAY

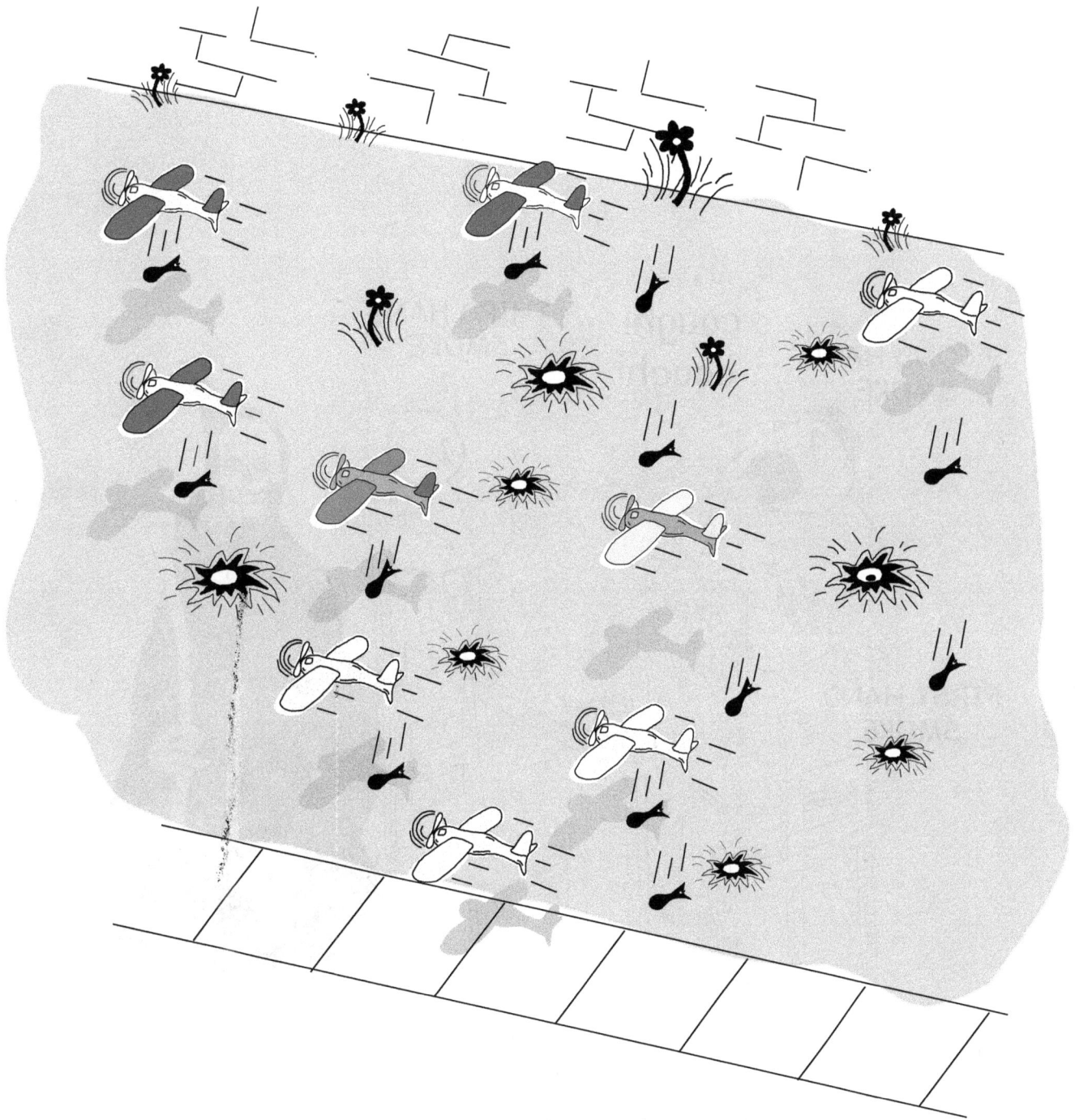

Even though Marvin wasn't sure
he believed what he was hearing,
he took his neighbor's advice and
began air-raiding his front lawn.

ANYONE FOR BRIDGE?

YOU CAN BE THE DUMMY.

CARTOON BASICS #32:

~~WHERE~~ ~~HOW~~ TO DRAW THE LINE

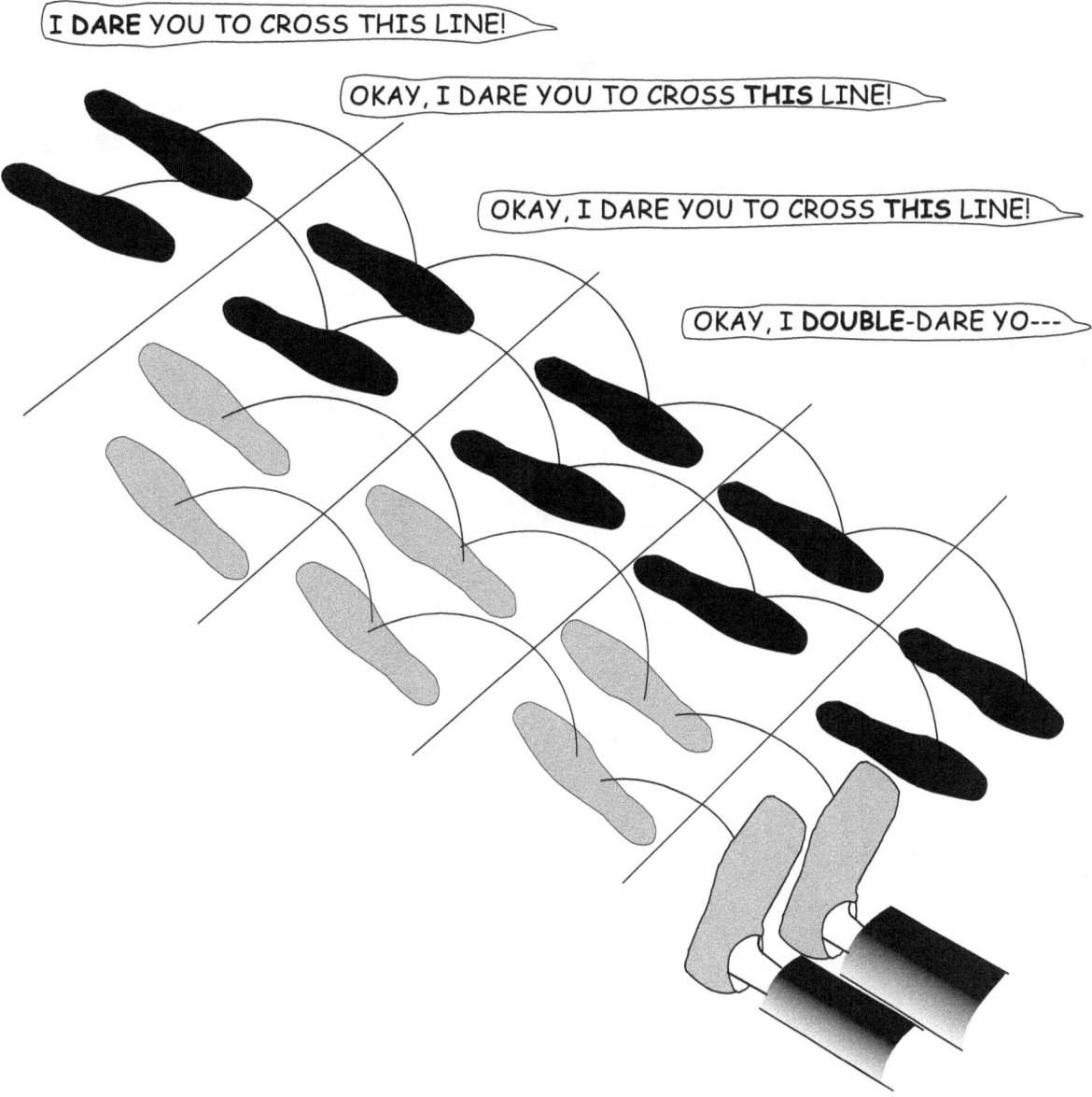

I **DARE** YOU TO CROSS THIS LINE!

OKAY, I DARE YOU TO CROSS **THIS** LINE!

OKAY, I DARE YOU TO CROSS **THIS** LINE!

OKAY, I **DOUBLE**-DARE YO---

CARDIAC ARREST

WELCOME TO
INCOGNITO
POPULATION:
WHO WANTS TO KNOW?
NO, I DON'T KNOW
WHO WE ARE EITHER.

KOWTOWING

*APOLOGIES TO GARY LARSON

ECONOMICAHOLICS ANONYMOUS

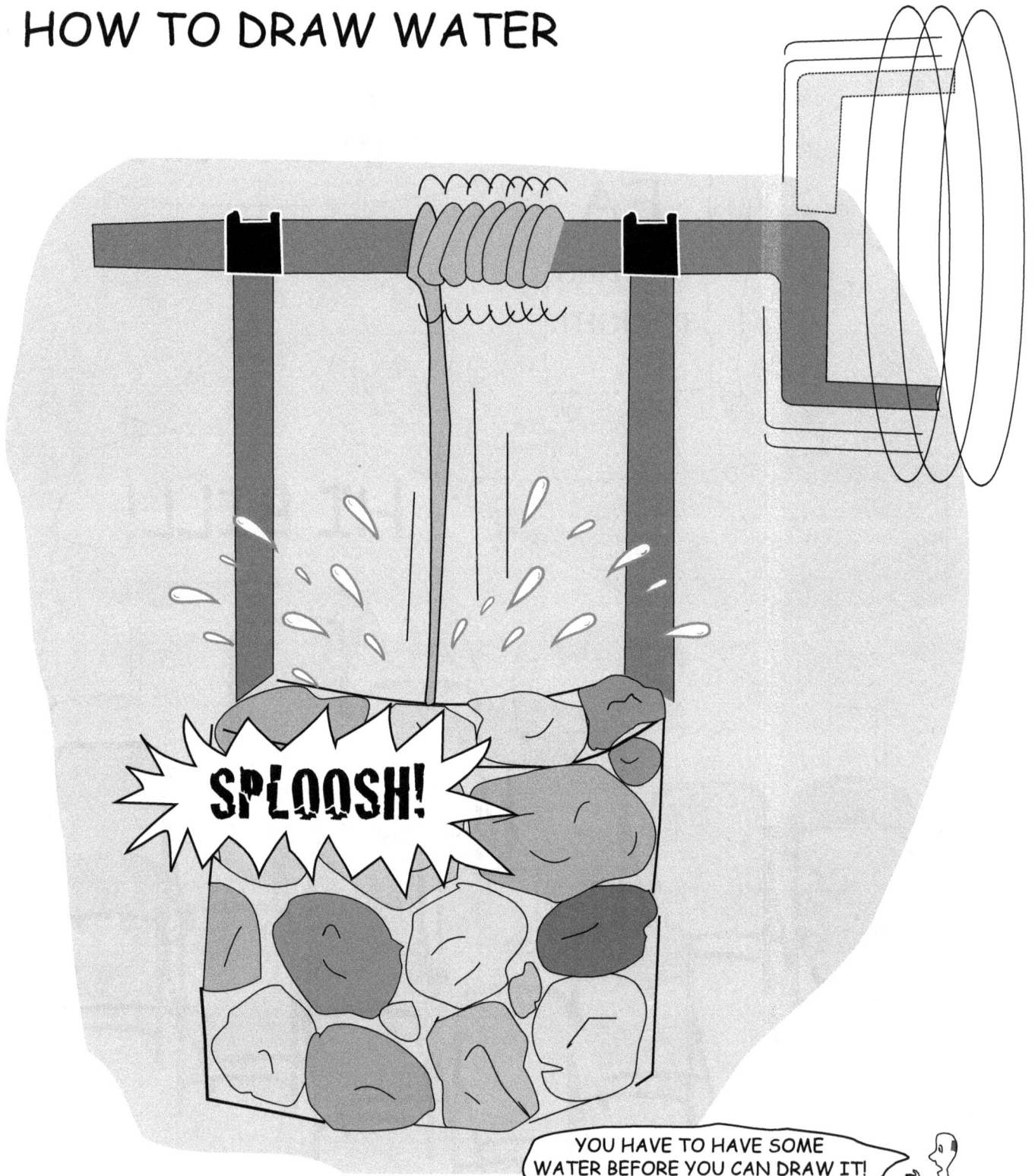

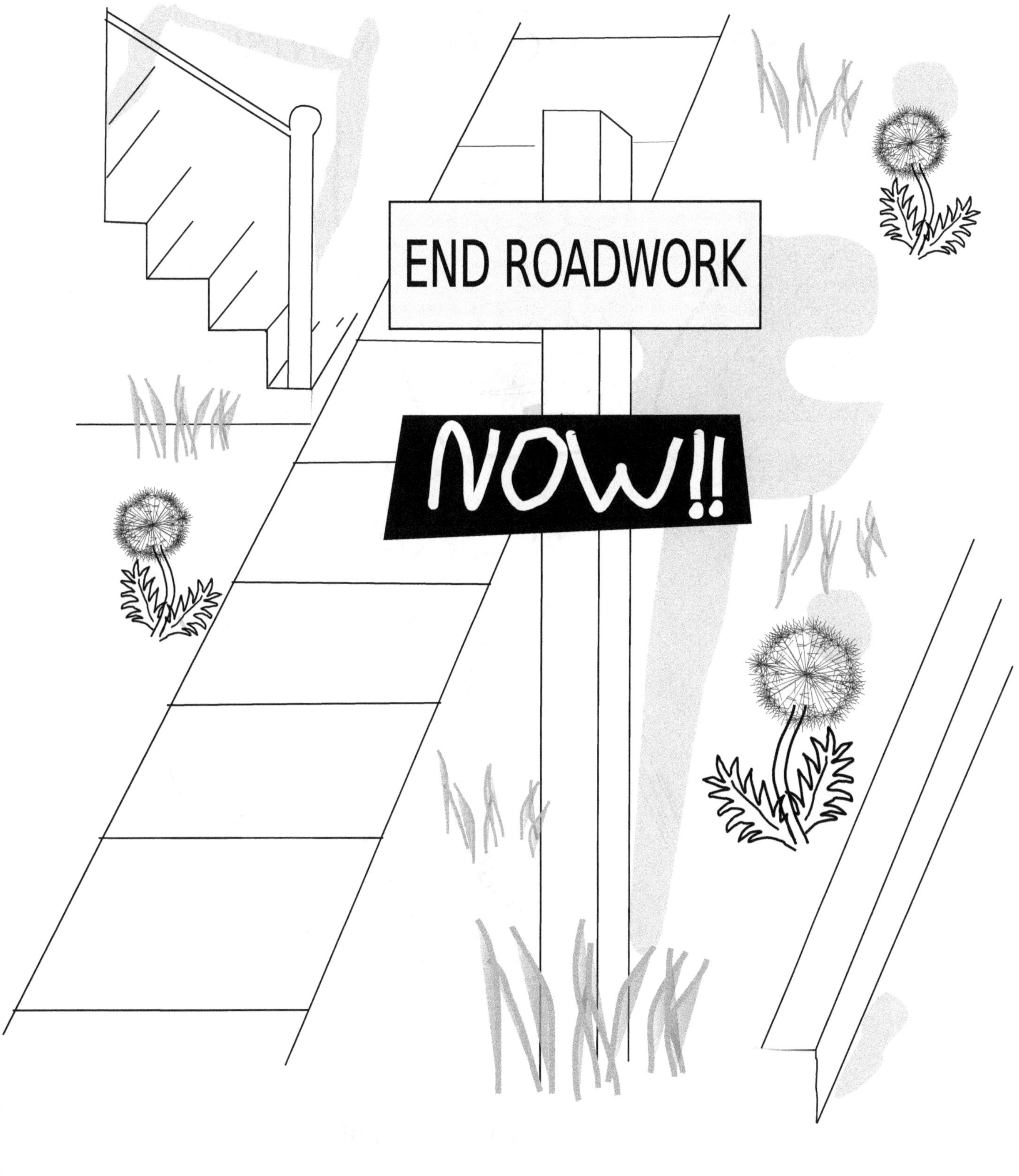
END ROADWORK
NOW!!

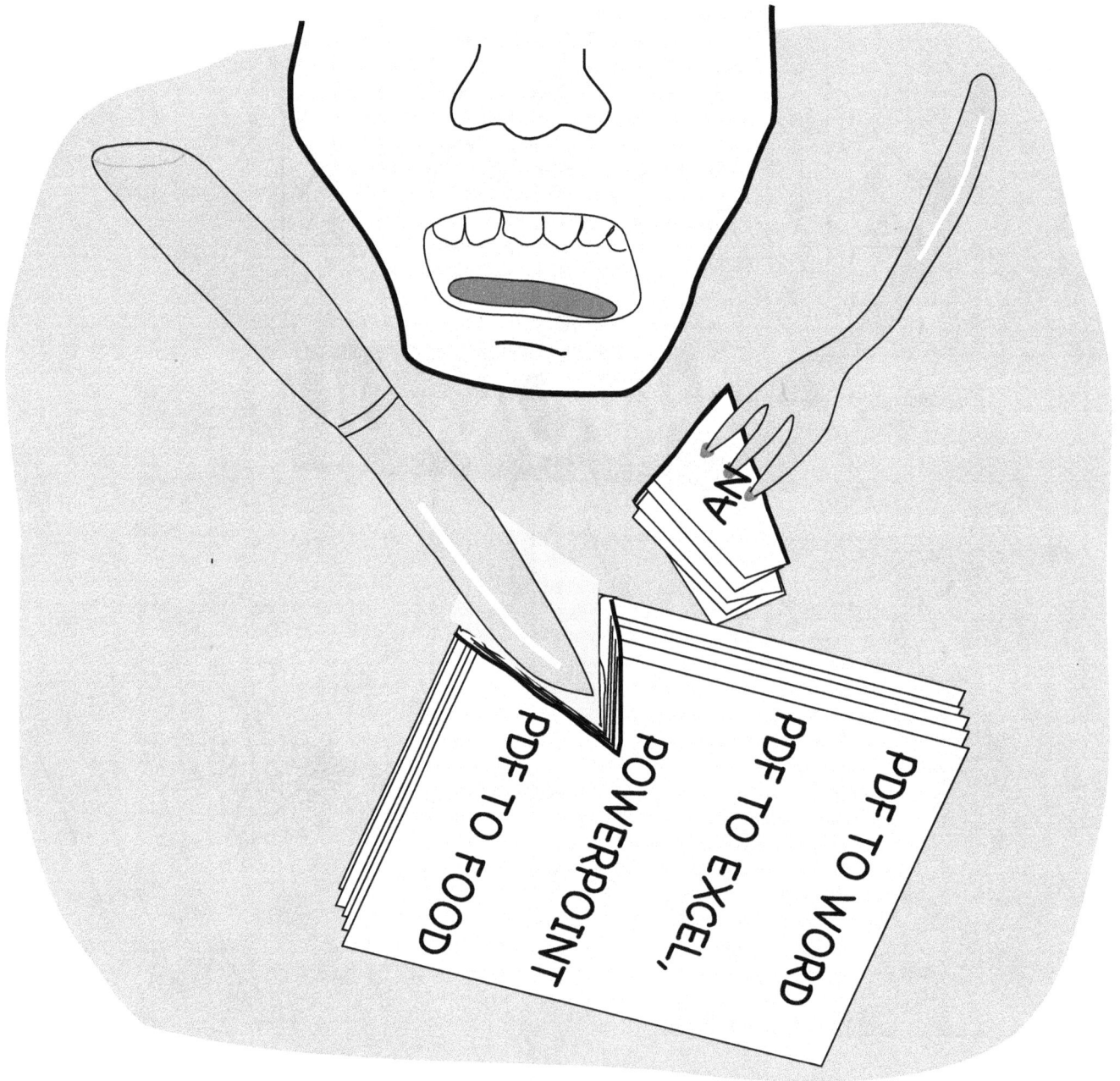

THE TERRORISTS MAKE A SERIOUS MISTAKE
STEALING HIGHLY-ENRAGED URANIUM

NOW, DANCE!

ENVIRON-MENTALIST IN ACTION

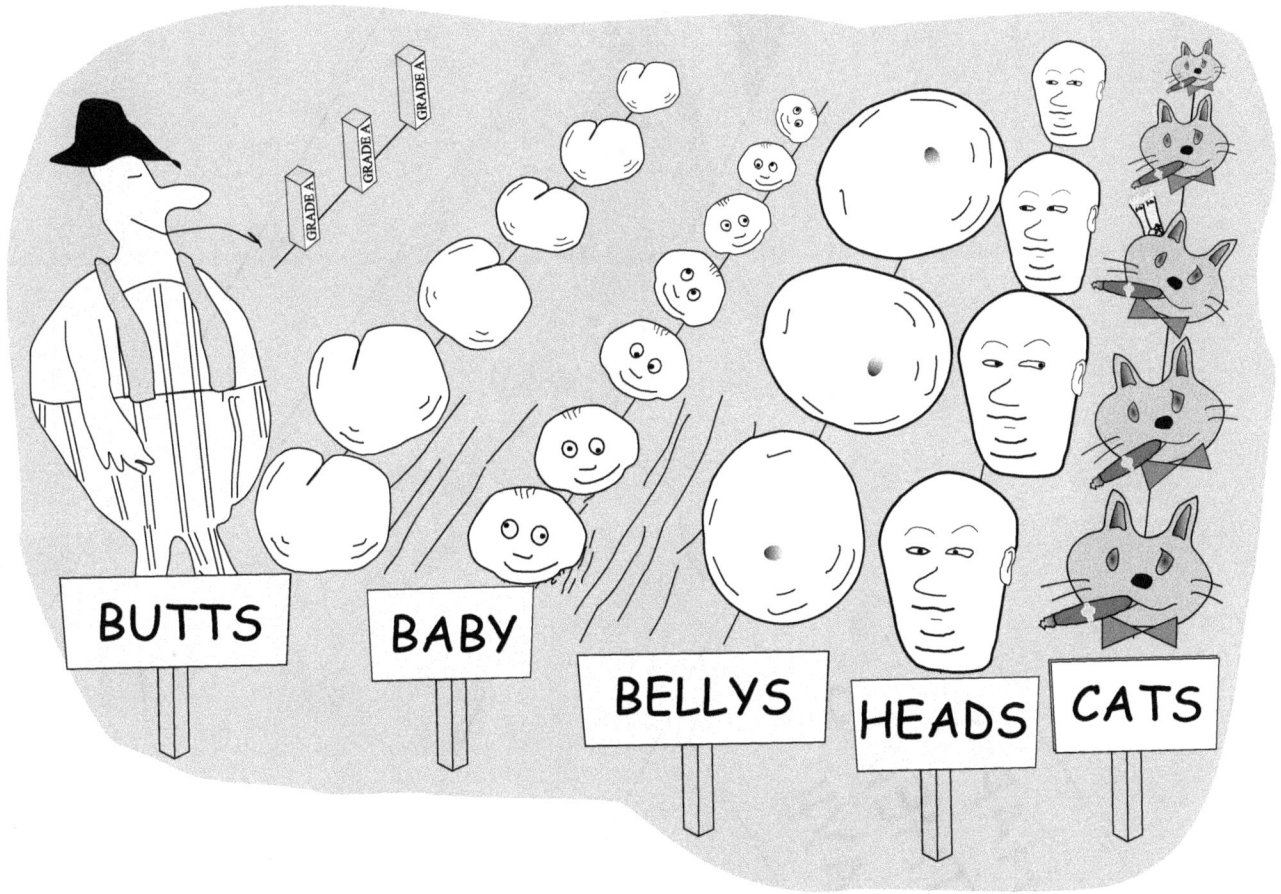

GRADE A GRADE A GRADE A

BUTTS BABY BELLYS HEADS CATS

FAT FARM

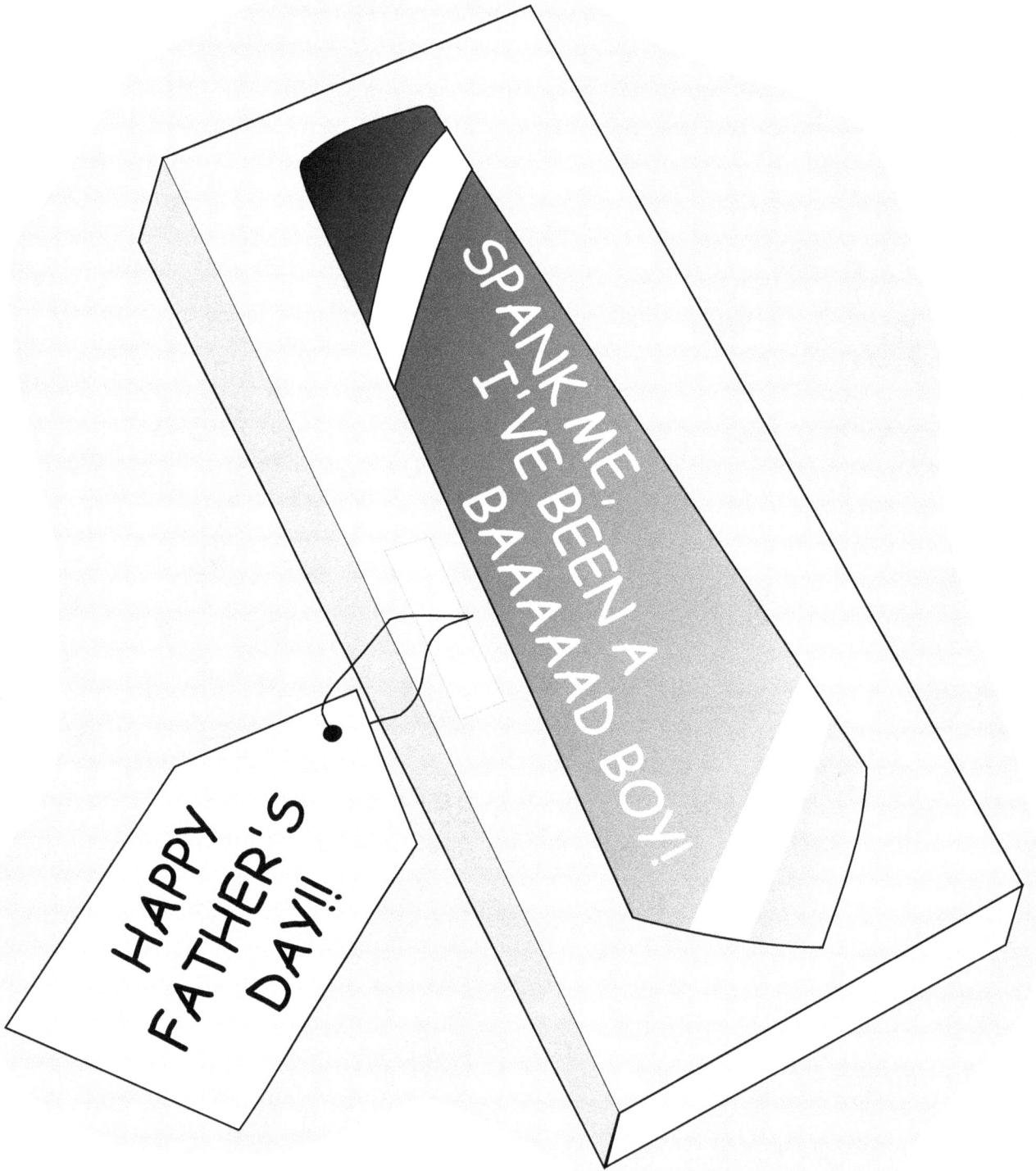

FAUX PA

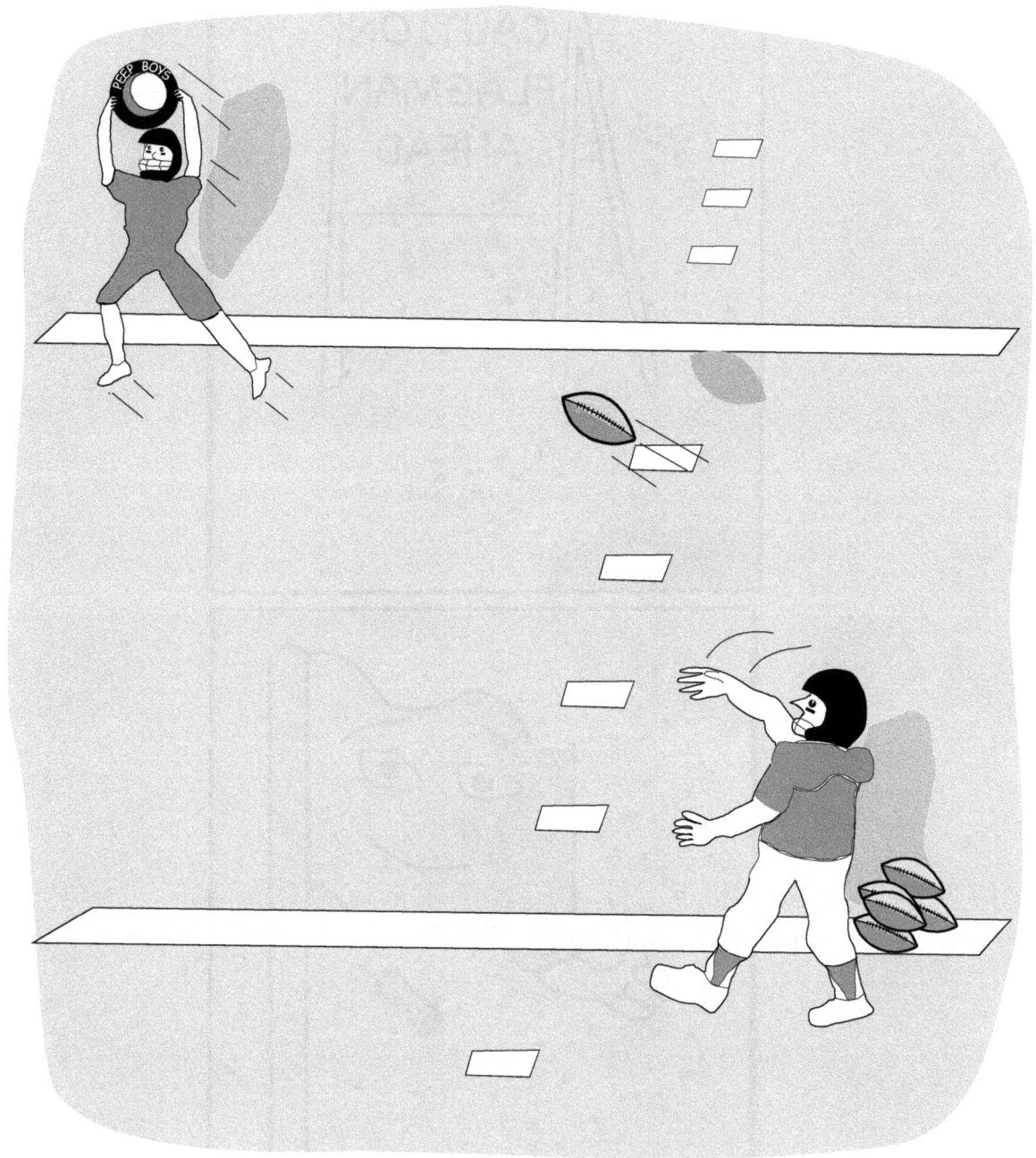

IT'S WHAT HE'S USED TO.

"HERE IN YELLOWSTONE PARK, WE HAVE THE LARGEST NUMBER OF 'ACTIVE' GEEZERS IN THE WORLD."
David Attenborough

HEY, SHOW US YOUR CUBES!!

SPRING BREAK FOR GLACIERS

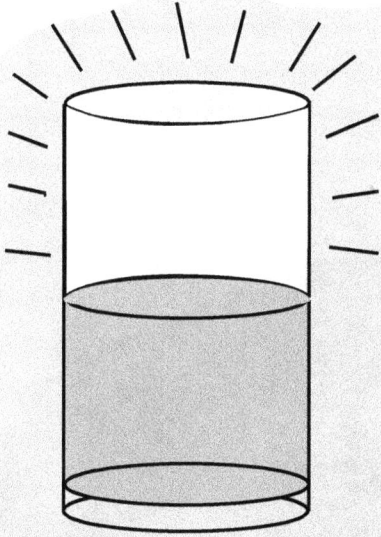

PESSIMISTS SEE THE
GLASS AS HALF EMPTY.

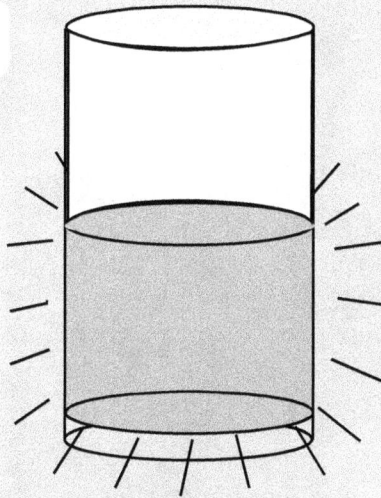

OPTIMISTS SEE THE
GLASS AS HALF FULL.

MY GLASS IS BROKEN.

STOP

CROSS TRAFFIC
DOES NOT STOP

HAPPY TRAFFIC
SLOWS DOWN
A LITTLE

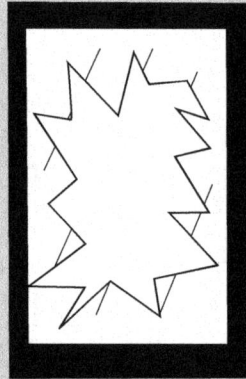

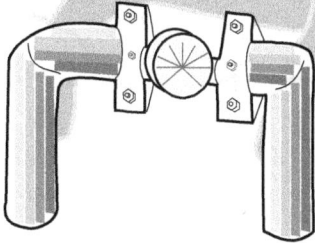

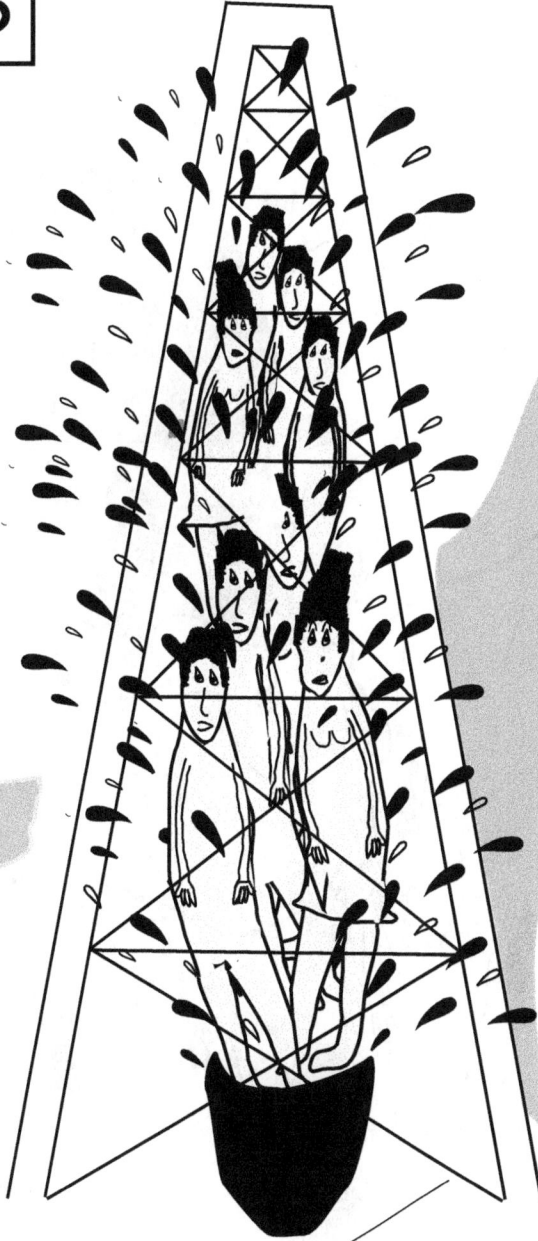

WELCOME TO
SCENIC HAMSTERDAM!

A CONJUGATIONAL VISIT

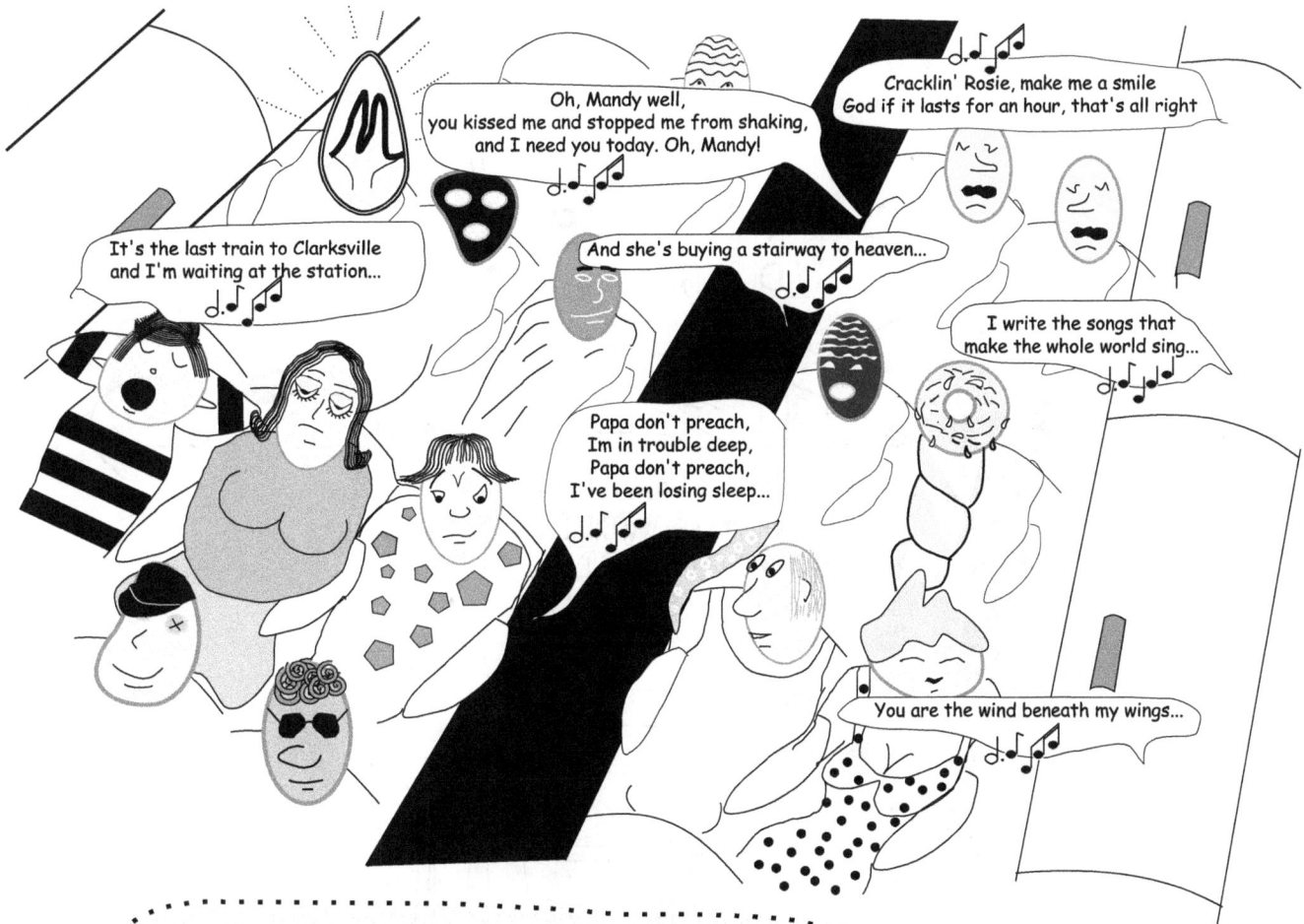

KARAOKE LUGGAGE

KIDNAPPERS AT HOME

LASSIE COMES THROUGH AGAIN!

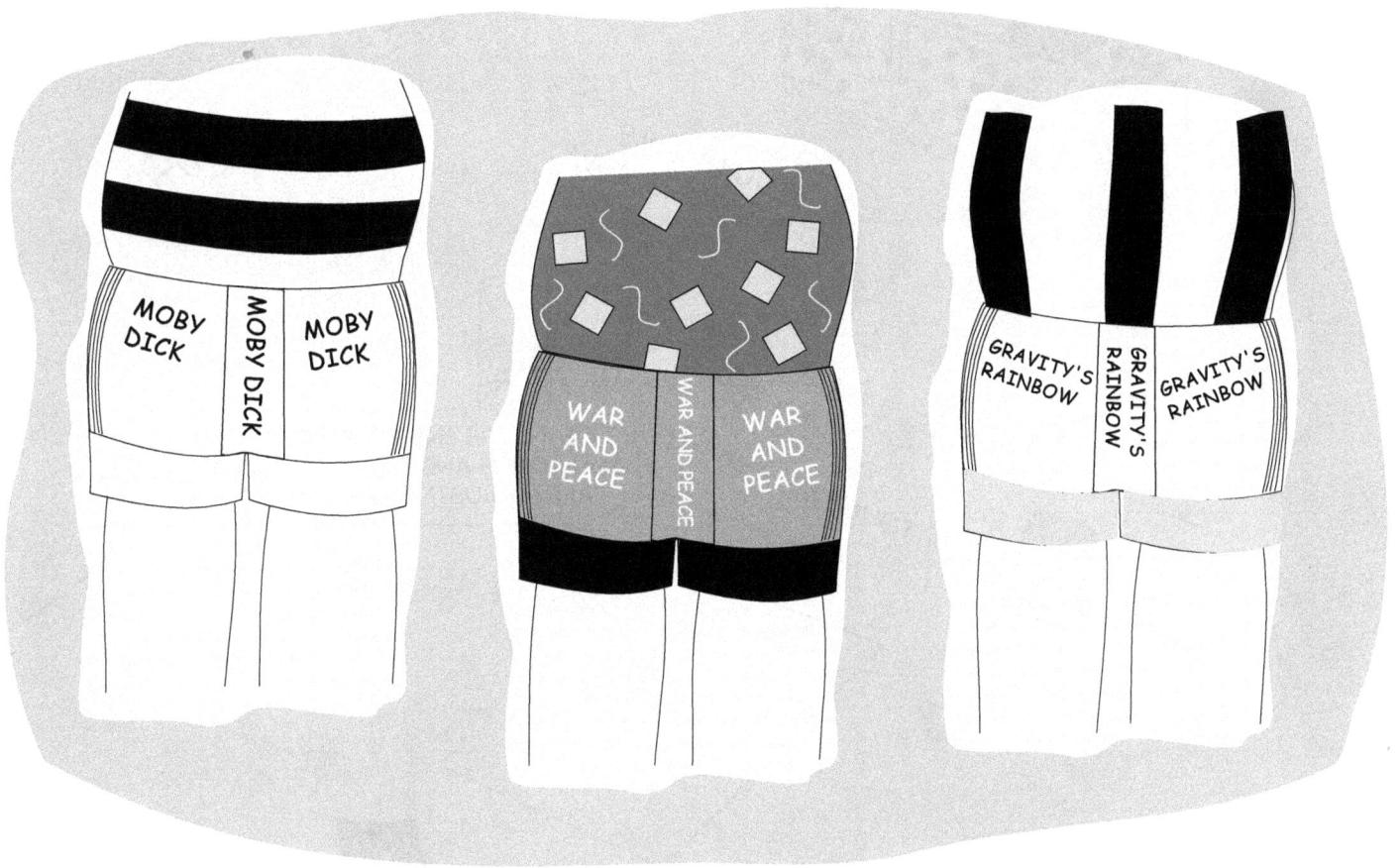

LONG STORY SHORTS

MASSAGYNIST

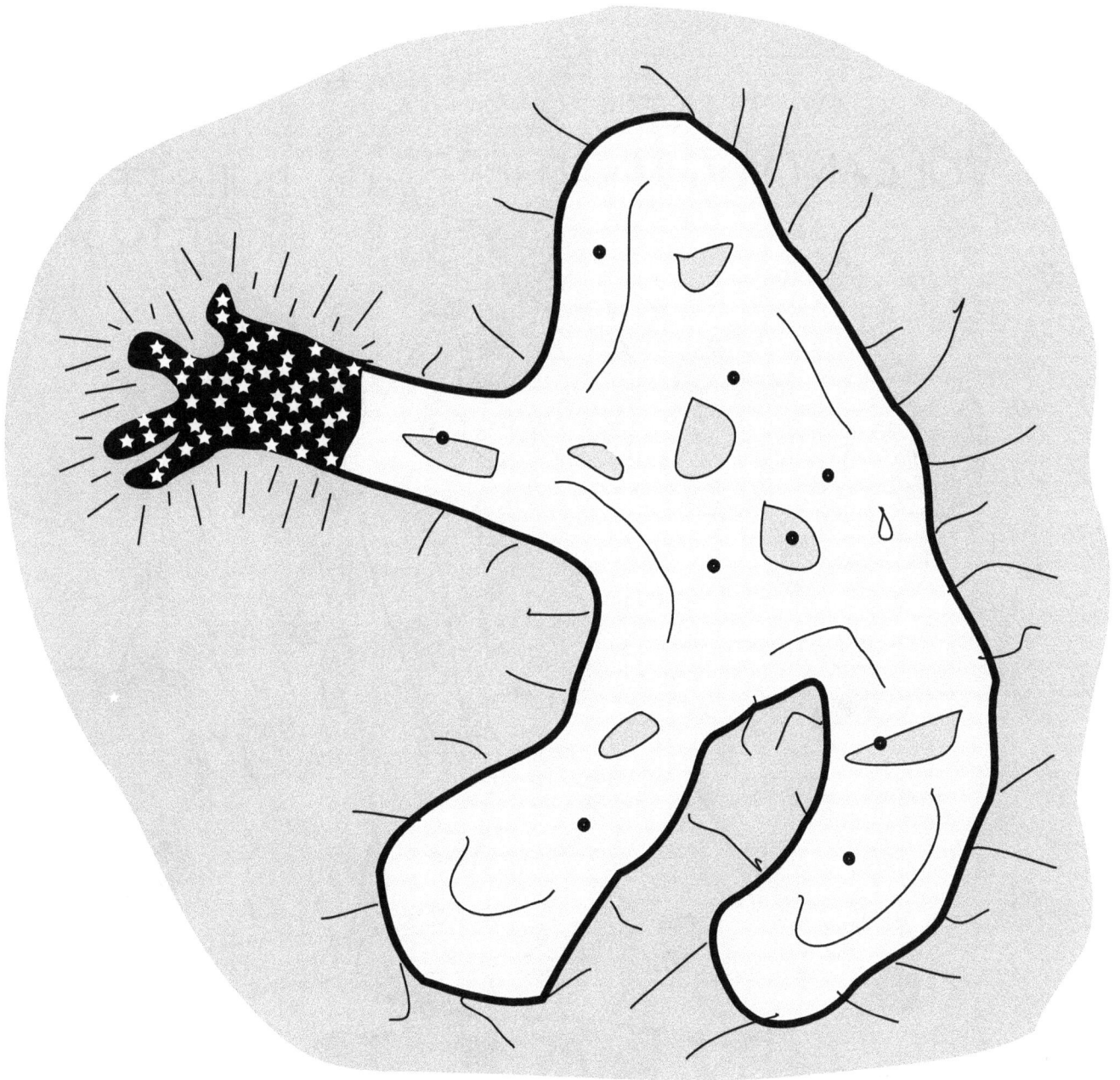

MICROBE JACKSON

NAUGHTY PINE

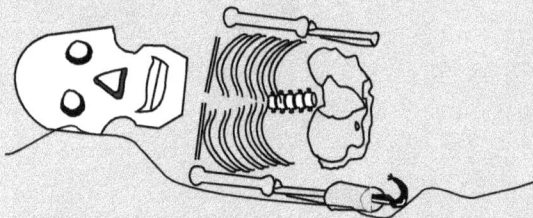

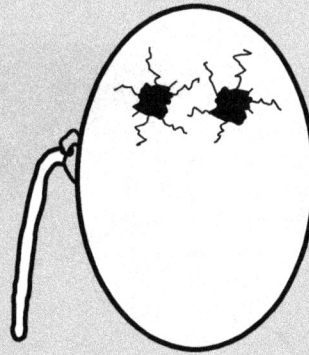

THE INCREDIBLE OEDIPAL EGG!

OOEY, GOOEY AND SPITOOEY,
DONALD'S OTHER NEPHEWS,
WAIT IN THE GREEN ROOM FOR
THE CALL THAT NEVER COMES...

THE TODAY, TONIGHT AND TOMORROW SHOW!

SCHEDULED

GEORGE CLOONEY
LADY GAGA
PRESIDENT OBAMA
OOEY, GOOEY, AND
SPITOOEY?

SHOULD WE CALL UNCA' DONALD?

NO, LET'S WAIT A

FEW MORE DAYS.

THE LEGEND OF PAUL'S BUNION

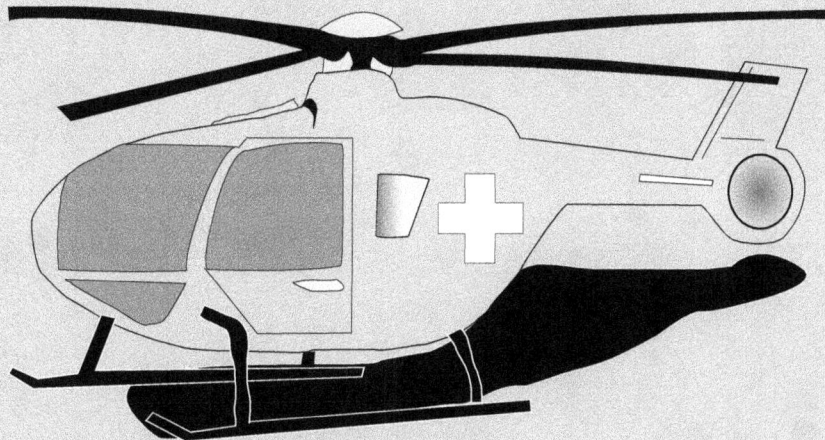

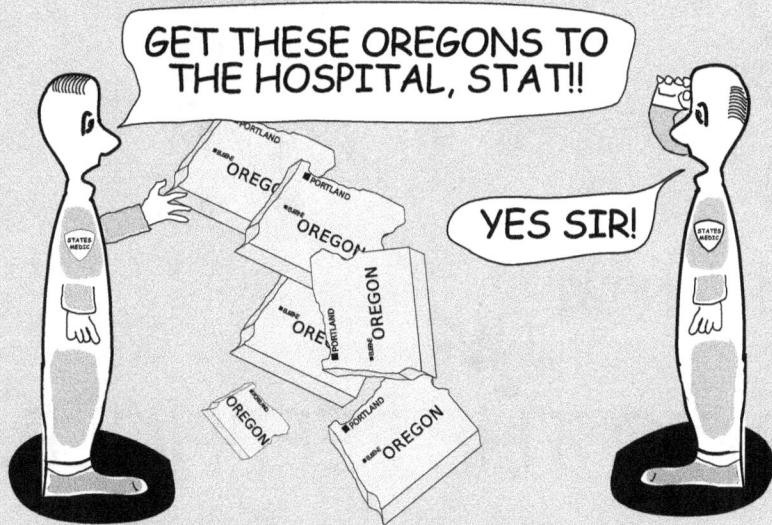

REPEAT THE WORD, SPELL THE WORD, AND GIVE THE DEFINITION. THE WORD IS 'PERUSE".
PERUSE. P-E-R-U-S-E... MORE THAN ONE PERU.
SPELLING BE
CORRECT!

PETER PAN IS APPALLED WHEN HE DISCOVERS THE SOURCE OF "FAIRY DUST"!?!

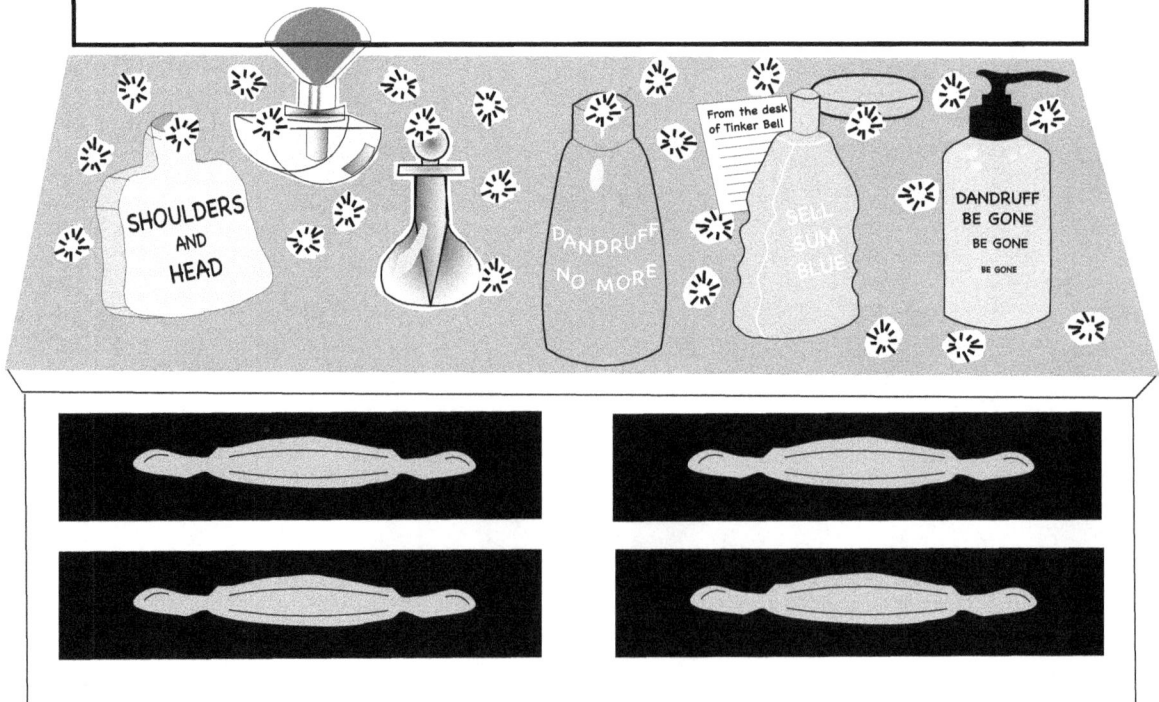

http://www.popupsaregoodforyou.com/youbet

AYE MATEYS, BE SURE TO CHECK OUT OUR WEBSITE, PIRATES.ARG!

END SCHOOL ZONE
PLEASE RESUME DRUG-DEALING, PROSTITUTION, AND SMOKING

RLS MIDNIGHT FUN RUN

SUFFER FROM <u>EXTREME</u> RESTLESS LEG SYNDROME?

HOW TO STOP A CHARGING RHINO

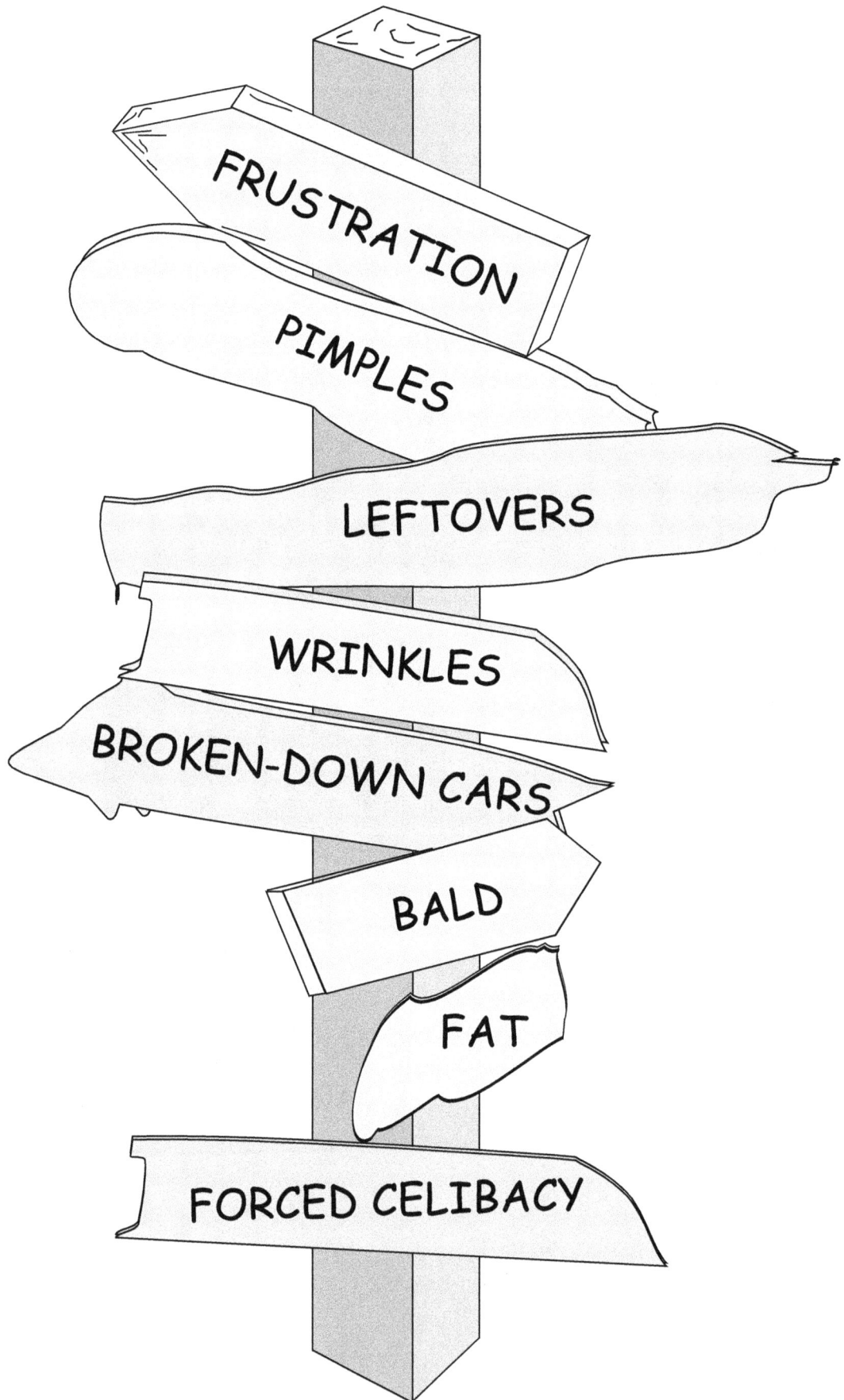

SIGNS OF LIFE

SILENT AUCTION

FRESH DODO DROPPINGS

FRESH DODO
DROPPINGS

.50
5.50
5.80
$11

UNBROKEN WIND

UNBROKEN WIND

1.00

75¢

A MOOT POINT

A MOOT POINT

5
6
9
10
12

SLICE OF THE OZONE LAYER

SLICE OF THE
OZONE LAYER

.50
5.50
5.80
$11
$12
$15
$100
$101

**AIR GUITAR
used by Mick Jagger**

AIR GUITAR
used by Mick Jagger

.50
5.50
5.80
$1100
$1200
$1500
$10000
$10100

THE EMPEROR'S NEW CLOTHES

THE EMPEROR'S
NEW CLOTHES

.50
5.50
5.80
$11
$12
$15
$100
$101

ANOREXIC'S DINNER

ANOREXIC'S DINNER

$1

**SONGS OF
MARCEL MARCEAU**

SONGS OF
MARCEL MARCEAU

$100
110
115
200
210

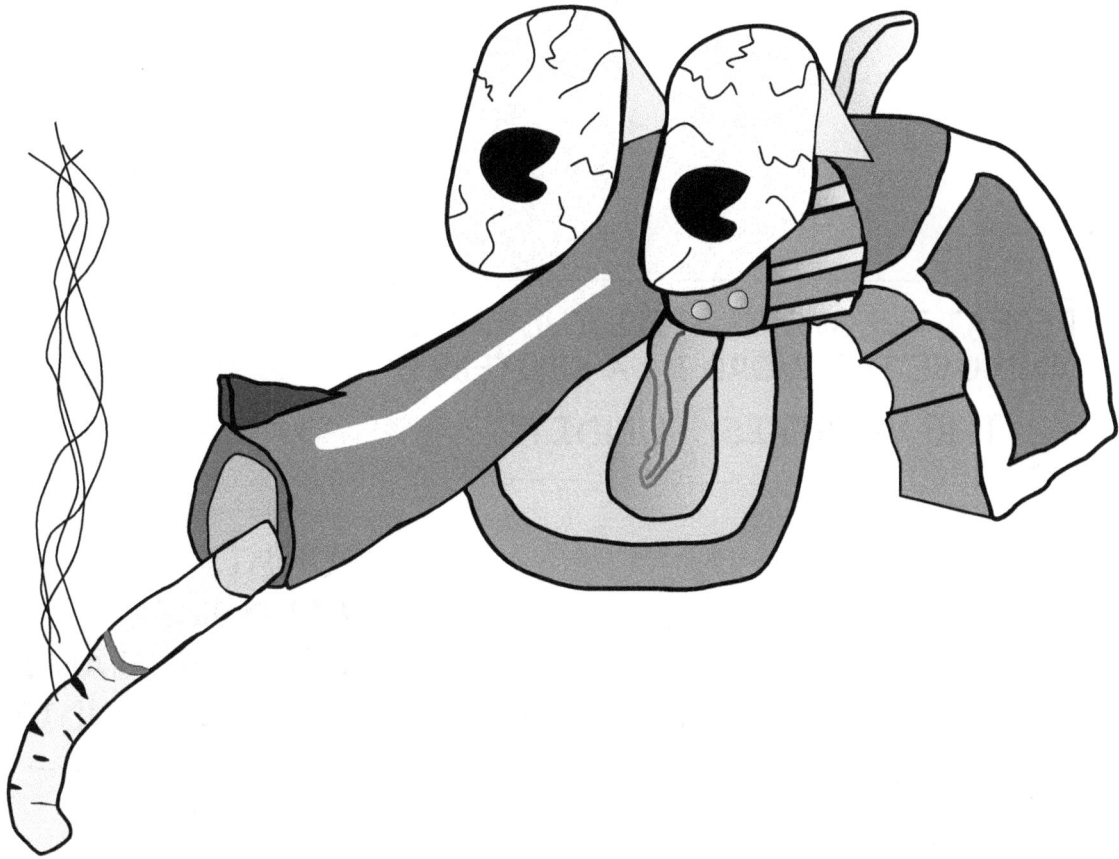

"WELL... WE FINALLY FOUND THE SMOKING GUN!"

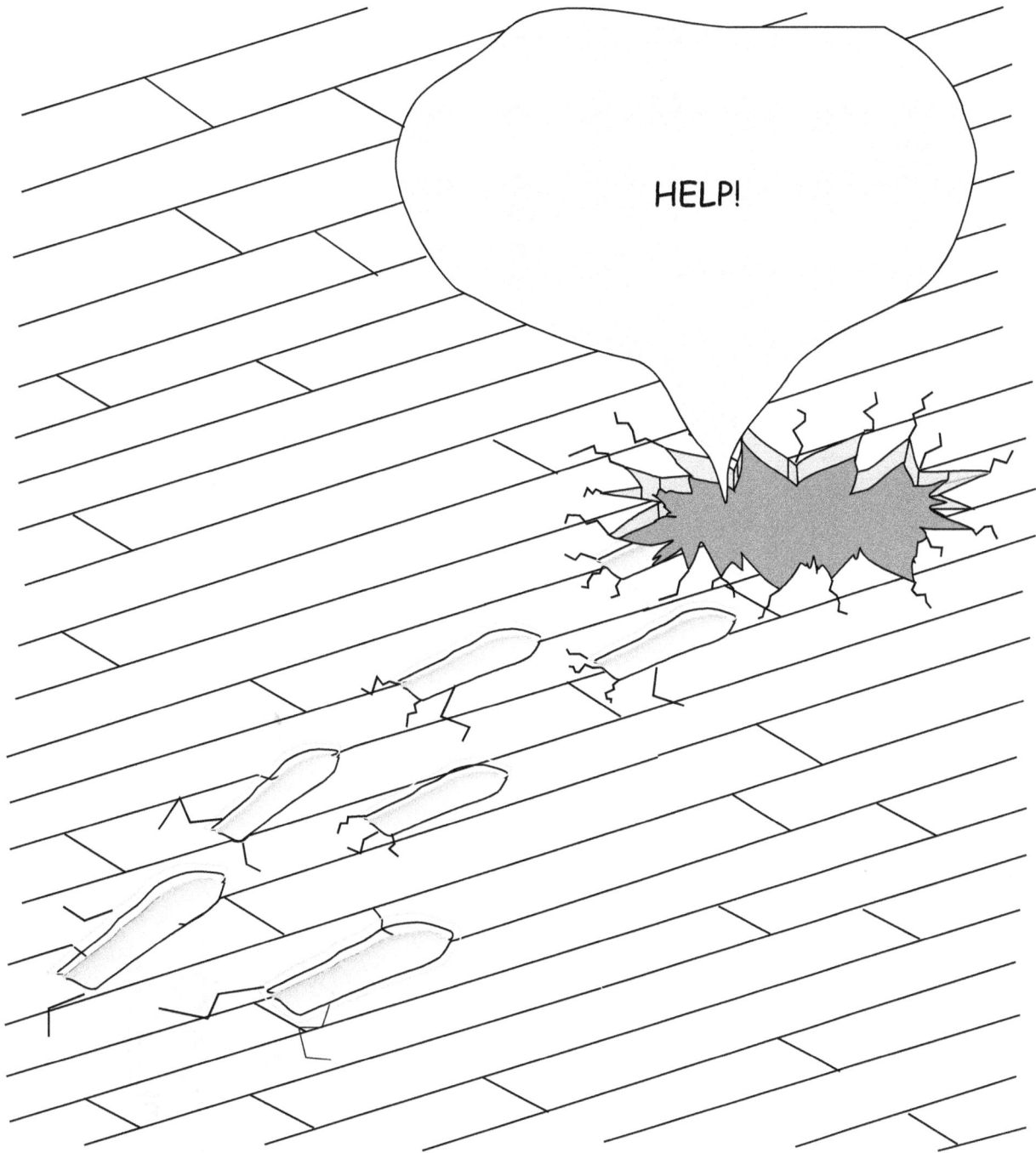

WHY SOFTWOOD FLOORS AREN'T SO POPULAR

THE EFFECT OF STOOL SOFTENER

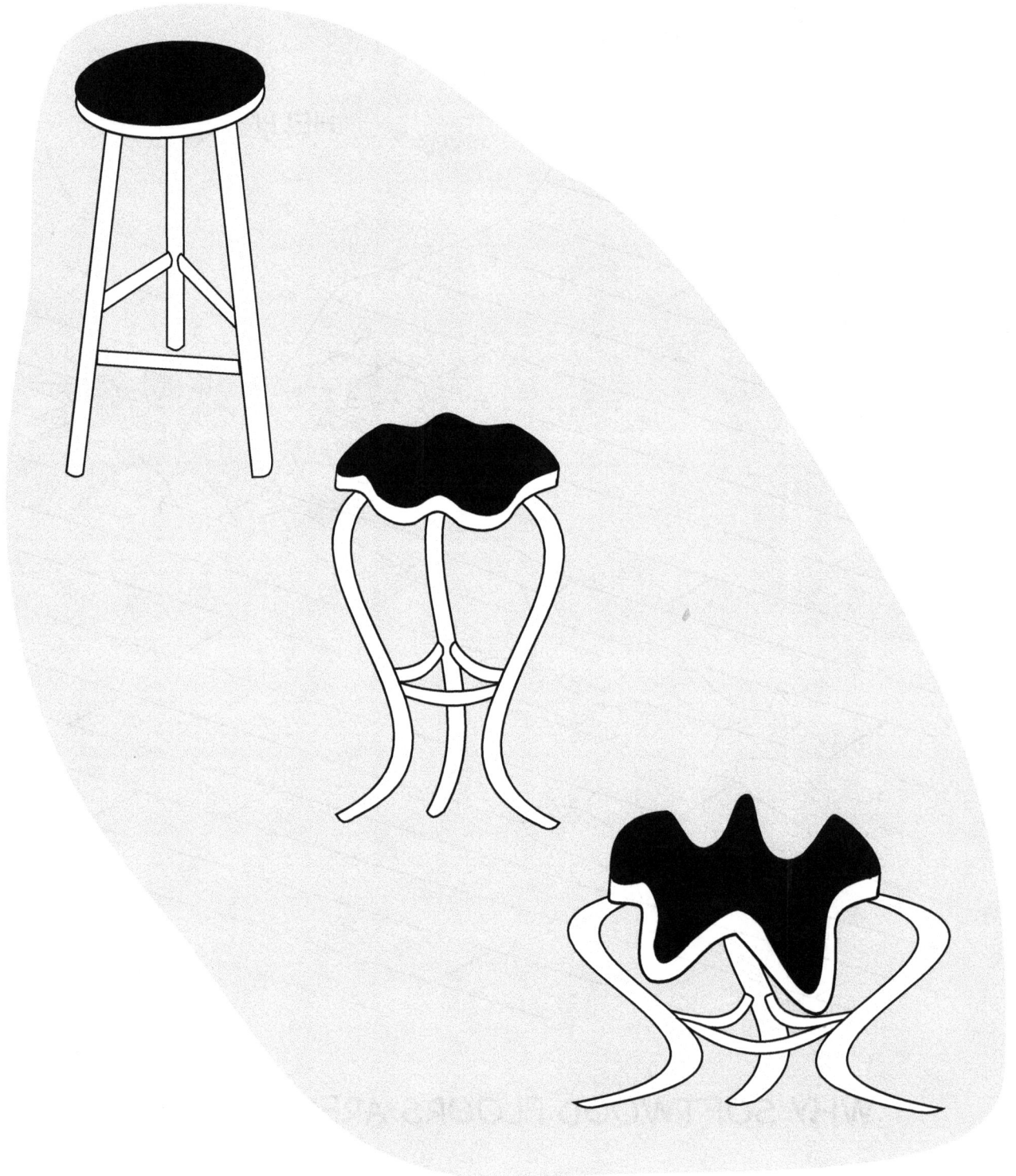

THE SUICIDE WATCH

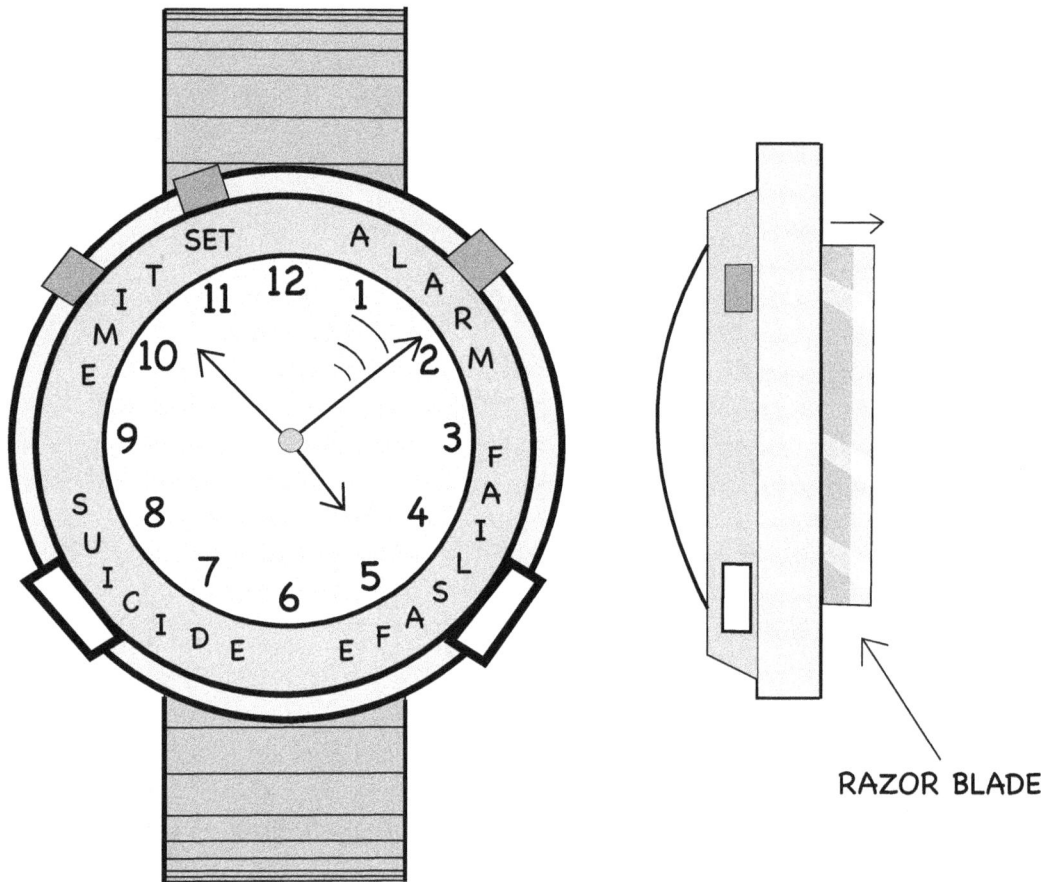

RAZOR BLADE

WHEN YOU WANT TO
KILL MORE THAN TIME.

THE PERFECT STOCKING-STUFFER!

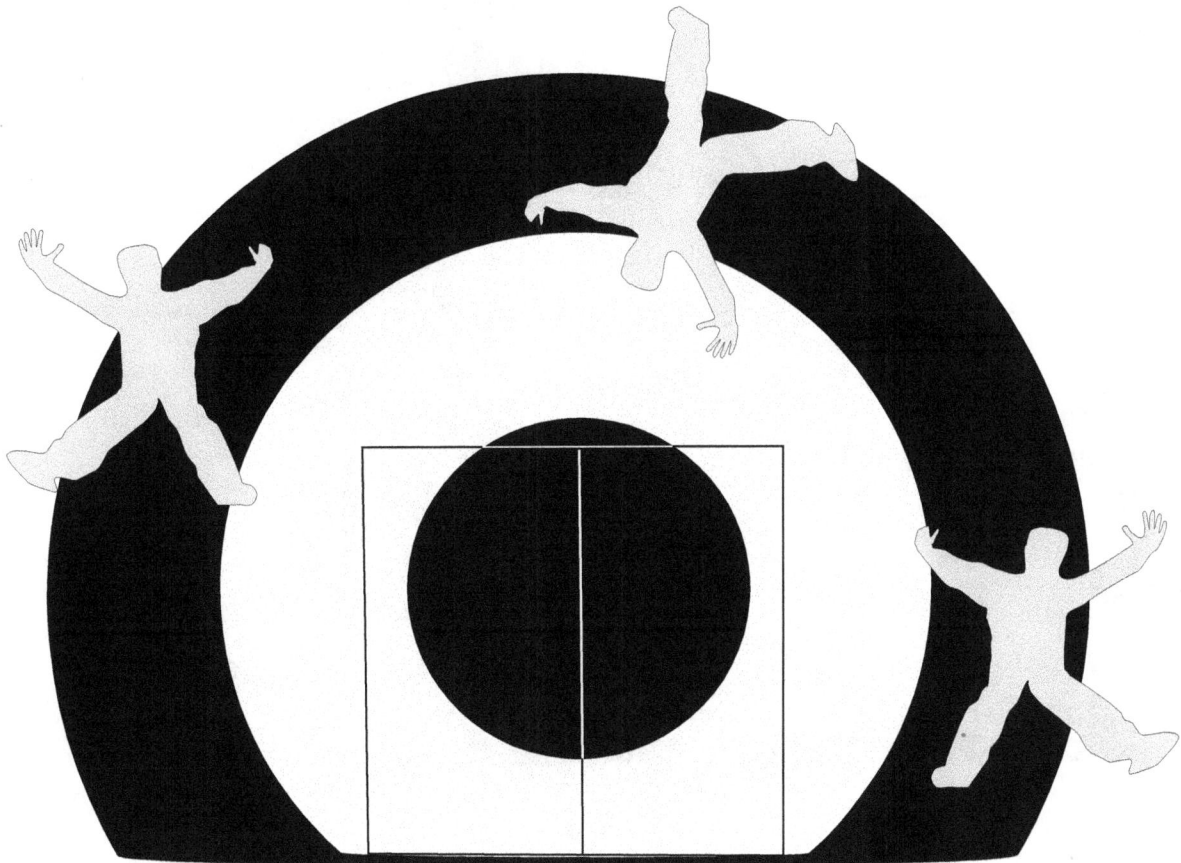

UNSUCCESSFUL TARGET SHOPPERS

Mitch Hedburg

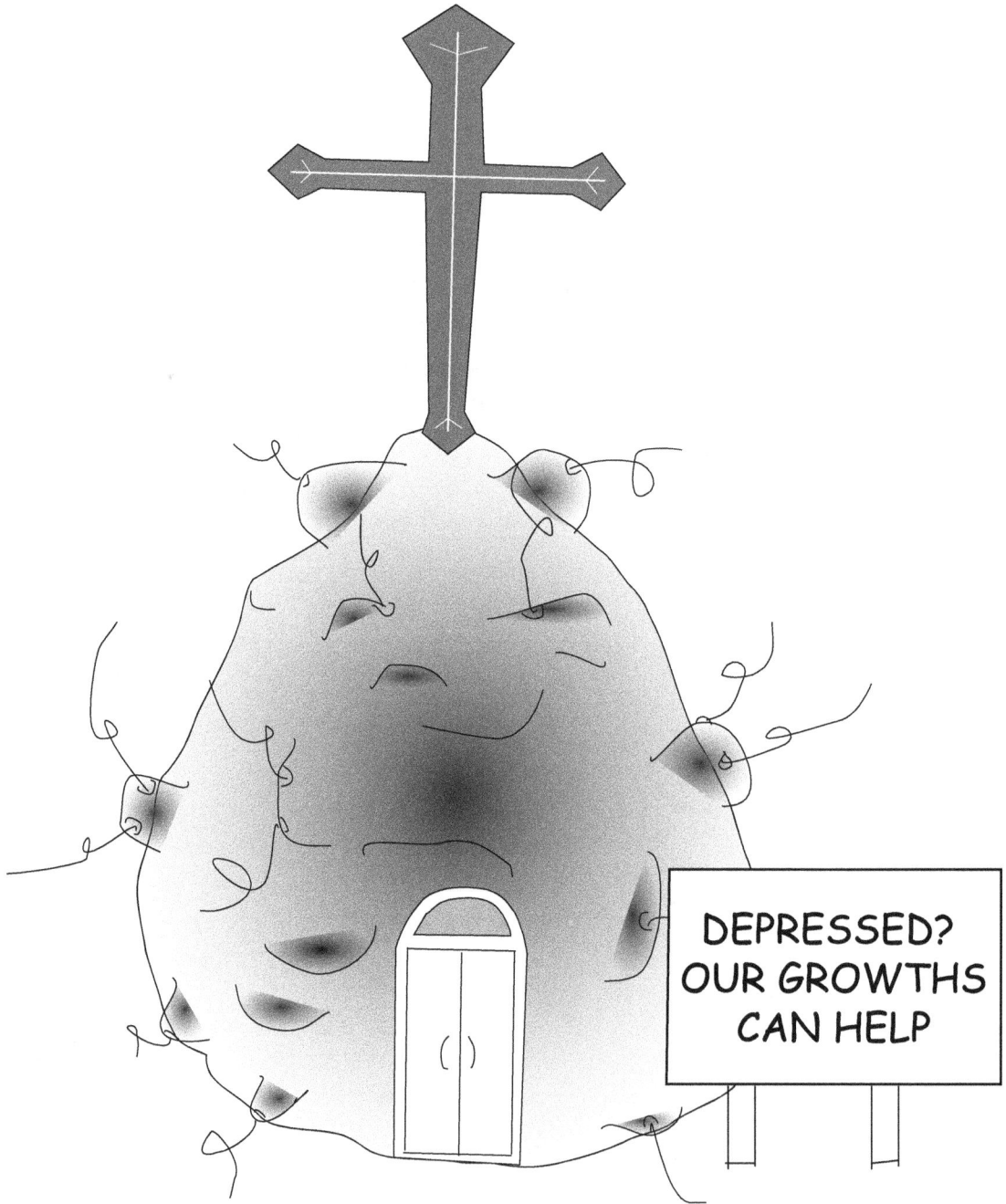

DEPRESSED?
OUR GROWTHS
CAN HELP

THE CHURCH OF ST JOHN'S WART

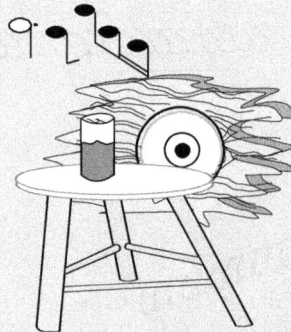

THE LONE RANGER AND TONTO,
HIS FAITHFUL INDIAN PSYCHIC

HOW GLOBAL WARMING AFFECTS US ALL...

SUPERMAN LONGS FOR THE DAYS WHEN HIS
FORTRESS OF SOLITUDE WASN'T SO DAMP...

THE MAKERS OF THE SUICIDE WATCH PROUDLY PRESENT

THE TORNADO WATCH

WHEN TIME ABSOLUTELY HAS TO FLY!

(COMING SOON, THE HURRICANE WATCH!)

ORGAN AND TISSUE DONATIONS

YES, THAT IS AN ORGAN AND THOSE ARE TISSUES...

UNCLEAR ON THE CONCEPT

PEACH COBBLER

RUBBERNECKERS

HELP DRESS THE DOLLY LLAMA

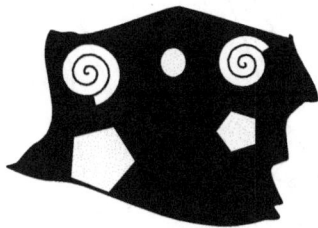

BABY SHOWER

HE LEFT SOME MIGHTY
BIG SHOES TO FILL!!

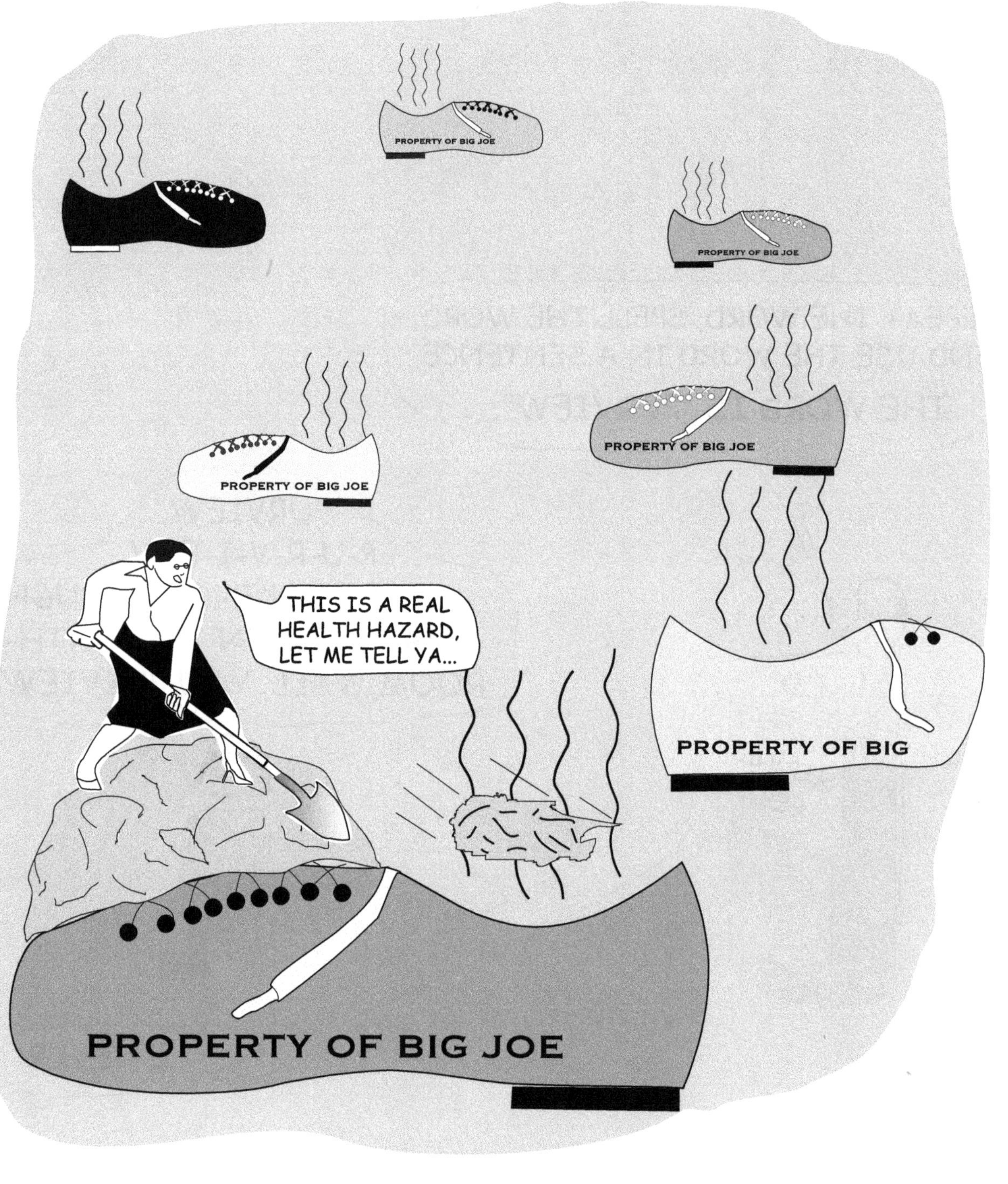

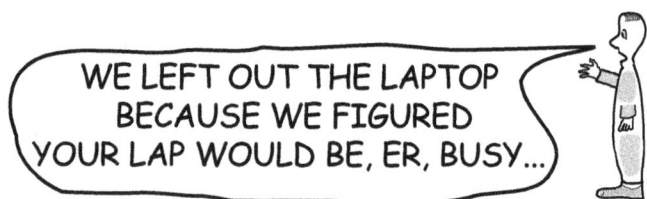

Intellectually Left Blank

THE CARTOONS

ON   THE

FOLLOWING

PAGES SHOULD

BE CONSIDERED

OFF

COLOR

YOU SHOULD

SKIP THEM

IF YOU ARE

EASILY OFFENDED.

THE OVERLY-PERSONAL COMPUTER

MOONROOF

THE CAR DESIGNED WITH
THE FRAT BOY IN MIND

MENSROOM AT THE CARNIVAL

MARTIN LUTHER KING JR.'S EARLY DREAMS

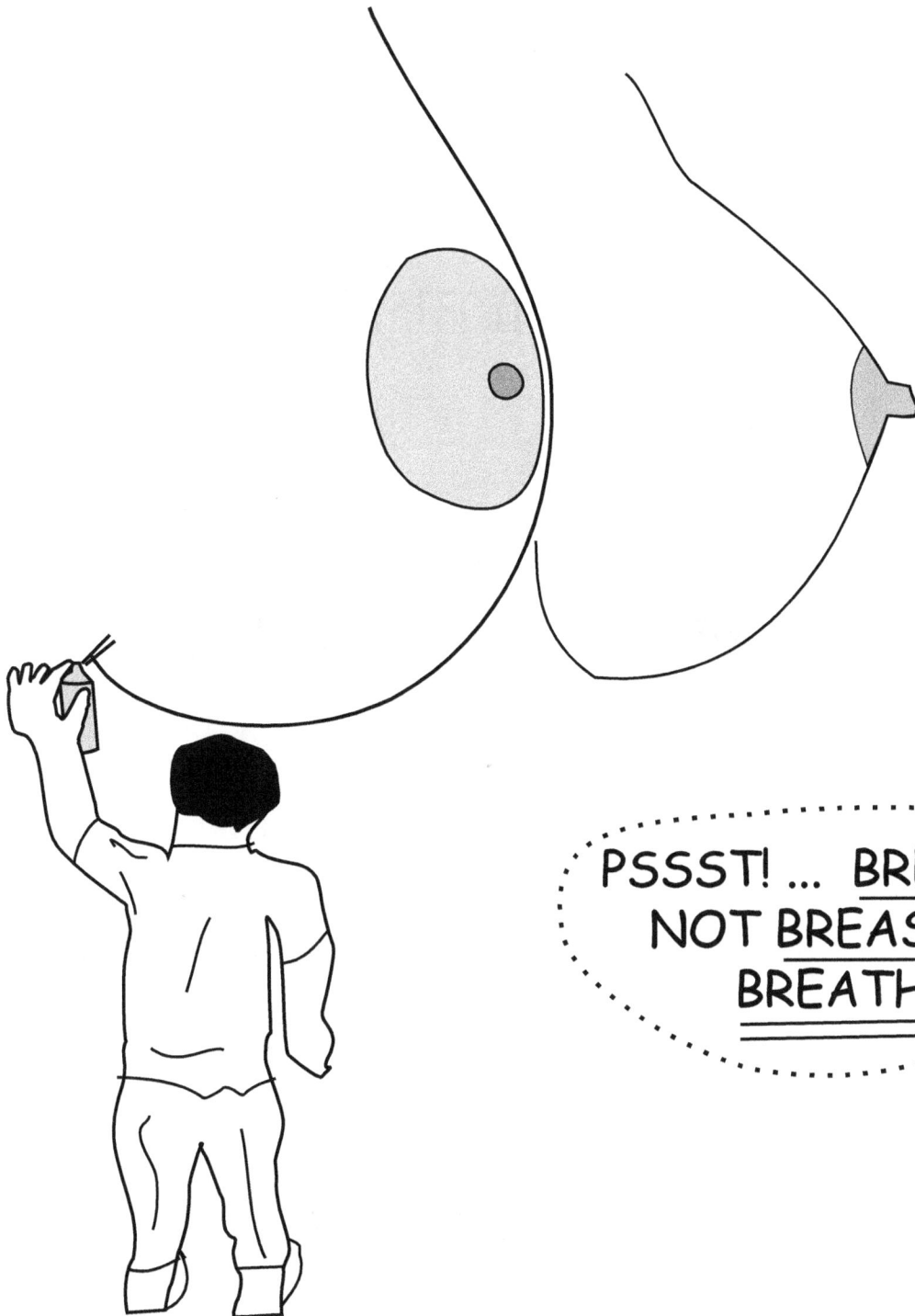

Ineffectually Left Blank

(Because,
as you can plainly see,
there are words on the page.)

THE PAIL

IF YOU ARE
NOT AN ADULT
DON'T GO...

BEYOND
THE
PAIL

THE MAN LOSES HIS YELLOW HAT...

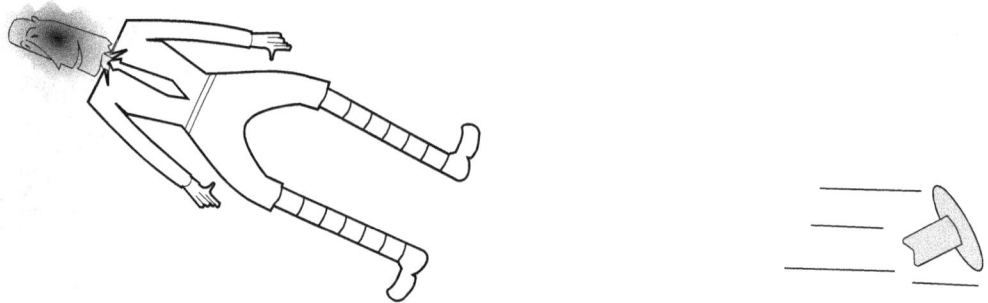

GEORGE THOUGHT, "WHAT'S UNDER THIS SKIN?"
GEORGE WAS CURIOUS.

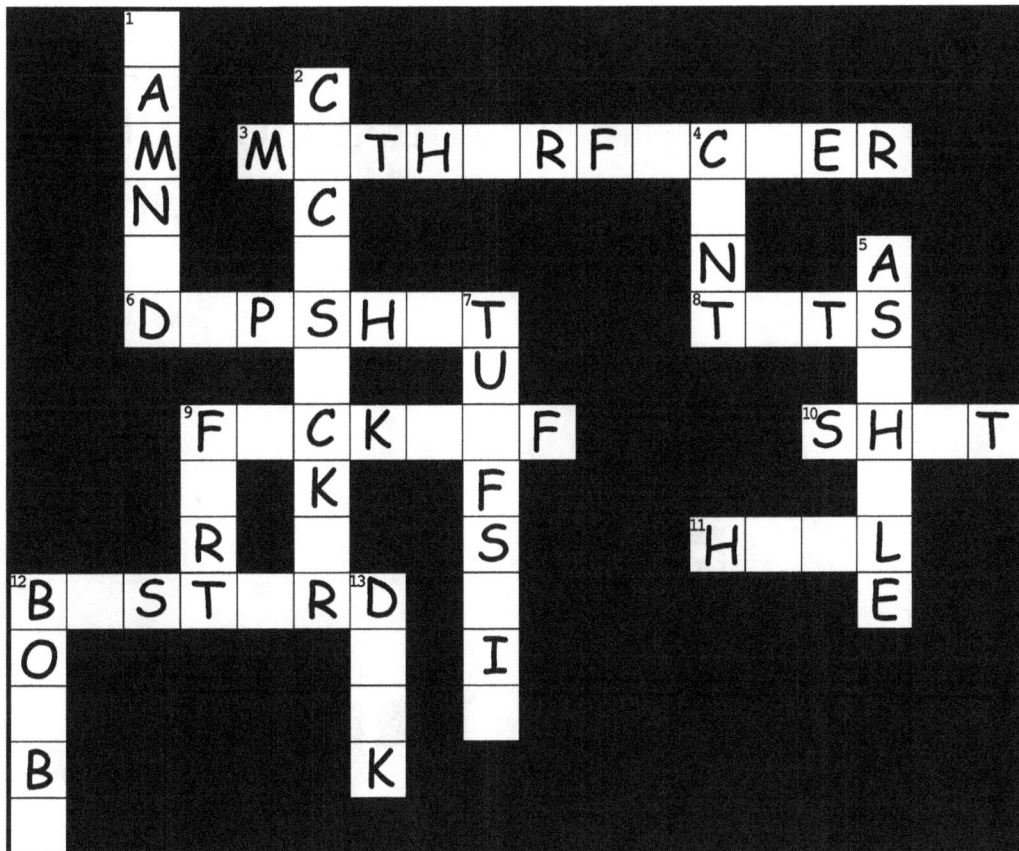

ACROSS

3 WHAT EVERY FATHER IS

6 IDIOT

8 THE BIGGER THESE ARE, THE BETTER

9 GO AWAY

10 INDUCED BY LAXATIVES

11 BAD PLACE TO CHILL

12 LOVE CHILD

DOWN

1 GOING TO HADES

2 BJ GIVER

4 CENTER OF THE UNIVERSE

5 BIG JERK

7 ACCEPT DISAPPOINTMENT

9 SILENT BUT DEADLY

12 LARGE ONES CAN TURN MEN INTO THESE

13 EVERY GUY'S GOT ONE

CUSSWORD PUZZLE

EXECUTIVES'
LAVATORY

MANAGEMENT'S CONCEPTION
OF EMPLOYEES' GOLDEN PARACHUTE

WHILE DREAMING OF BOTH
LOIS LANE AND LANA LANG,
SUPERMAN KNOCKS OUT THE CNN SATELITE

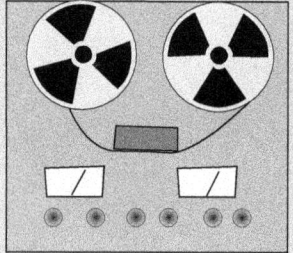

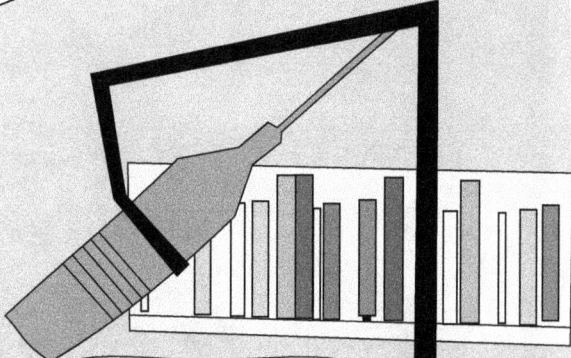

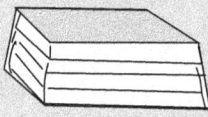

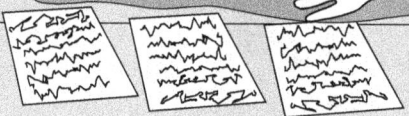

AN OLD-TIME MENSTRUAL SHOW

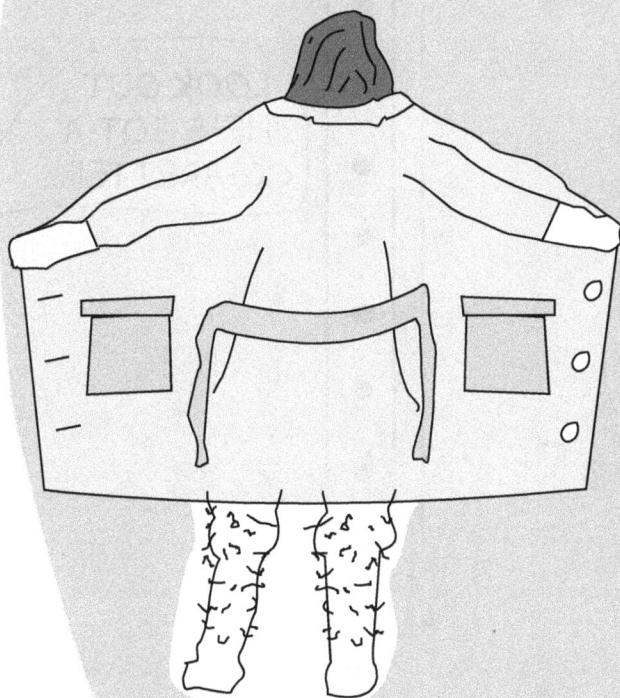

HALT OR I'LL SHOOT!!
THERE ARE DRUG DEALERS, GANGS, PIMPS, MUGGERS AND MURDERERS WHOM WE ALL NEED TO
BEWARE
BUT THE ONES WE REALLY NEED TO AVOID AT ALL COSTS ARE THE ONES WHO CAN KILL ANYONE, AT ANY TIME AND GET AWAY WITH IT, NO MATTER WHAT THE CIRCUMSTANCES, AND THAT'S THE
POLICE!
LOOK OUT , HE'S GOT A CIGARETTE!!...

Camphell's

JUNKY

LIP-SMACK-IN' GOOD

THE CATHETERIA:
ANOTHER IDEA
WHOSE TIME
WILL NEVER COME